The Chocolate Teapot

Surviving at school

David Lawrence

By the same author:
Killer Ping-Pong
The Superglue Sandwich
Travels with my Zebra
Big Questions about God and You
Help! My Parents are Aliens

Copyright © David Lawrence 1991, 2004

First published 1991

This revised edition published 2004
Reprinted 2004, 2007, 2010

ISBN 978 1 84427 051 4

Scripture Union, 207–209 Queensway, Bletchley, Milton Keynes, MK2 2EB,
England.
Email: info@scriptureunion.org.uk
Website: www.scriptureunion.org.uk

Scripture Union Australia
Locked Bag 2, Central Coast Business Centre, NSW 2252
Website: www.su.org.au

Scripture Union USA
PO Box 987, Valley Forge, PA 19482
www.scriptureunion.org

Except where otherwise stated, Scripture quotations are from the Good News Bible
published by The Bible Societies © 1966, 1971, 1976, 1992 American Bible Society.

British Library Cataloguing-in-Publication Data.

A catalogue record of this book is available from the British Library.

Printed by CPI Bookmarque, Croydon

Cover design: Martin Lore

Internal illustrations: Simon Smith

℘ Scripture Union is an international Christian charity working with churches
in more than 130 countries, providing resources to bring the good news about
Jesus Christ to children, young people and families and to encourage them to
develop spiritually through the Bible and prayer.
As well as our network of volunteers, staff and associates who run holidays,
church-based events and school Christian groups, we produce a wide range of
publications and support those who use our resources through training
programmes.

To Mark, Katheryn, Andrew, Liz, Tim and Emma
– a fine family of heatproof teapots.

Taking the lid off the chocolate teapot

There are lots of things that you can call a book. Here are some good names for books:

Hamlet

The Famous Five Go Roller Skating on Everest

My Little Donkey Annual 2004

Eric

Although these are all really good titles for books, this book is not called any of them. This book is called…

THE CHOCOLATE TEAPOT!!

Now of course it is obvious to you WHY this book is called *The Chocolate Teapot*. It isn't? Oh well, if you can't work it out for yourself I suppose I'd better tell you.

A teapot made of chocolate might look wonderful. It could be made to have a really ornate lid, interesting shape and long curving spout. You could even stuff it full of tea bags and all would be well, but the moment that the hot water is poured in disaster strikes and the chocolate teapot just melts away.

Sadly, this is a sort of picture of many young Christians. They look brilliant at church, at youth group – even sometimes at home! But when the going gets tough and the heat is on at school, they just melt away and merge with the crowd.

This book is for chocolate teapots everywhere; people who perhaps feel failures because they've never really managed to stand up at school for what they believe, or for people who would like to know a bit more about living for Jesus at school.

Contents

READ THIS! You don't have to read the chapters in any particular order. Start with the ones that are about the subjects which most interest you at the moment.

A barrel of laughs at Kidminster Green

(First day at secondary school)

'Now, let's just run through that list again.'

'Do we have to, Mum? We must have been through it ten zillion times already and I'm going to miss the bus.'

'Just once more, David. You don't want to get to your first day at Kidminster Green and discover that you've left something important behind, do you?'

'No, Mum.'

I had been packing and repacking my new school bag for the last week, so I knew that I had everything. But mums will be mums, so...

'Pencil case?'

'Yes.'

'Sports kit?'

'Yes.'

'Indoor *and* outdoor?'

'Yes.'

'Calculator?'

'Yes.'

'Dinner money?'

'Yes.'

'Craft apron?'

'Yes.'

'Snack for break time? You'll be hungry, you know.'

My bag already looked like a sumo wrestler in a sleeping bag.

I knew. 'Bag of crisps, Kit Kat and carton of Jolly Jim's Jungle Juice.'

Mum looked relieved. 'That should do you. What about your bus pass? Have you got your bus pass somewhere safe?'

'Yes, yes, yes. For goodness' sake, Mum. Even if I *have* forgotten something, there's no way I could carry anything else to school. My bag already looks like a sumo wrestler in a sleeping bag.'

'Well, are you sure you're happy to go on the bus? I could always take you in the car, you know.'

'NO! No… thanks all the same.' The thought of turning up for my first day at secondary school with Mum in tow was just too embarrassing to even think about.

Now what? She was looking at me in a weird kind of way.

'You OK, Mum?' I asked.

'Oh, just look at you. You look so smart in your new uniform. Proper grown up. I was just thinking how…'

I interrupted. 'Wow, look at the time. Must rush for the bus.' If Mum was getting into sentimental mode, it was time to make a sharp exit.

As I ran down the path, I could still hear her giving it all she'd got. 'Be polite. And don't be afraid to ask questions. Just do your best, you can't do more than that. And don't forget where to catch the bus home. And keep your dinner money safe. And keep well away from any trouble. And…'

The bus ride was uneventful, and it wasn't long before I arrived at the school gates. I knew what I was supposed to do next because I had already visited the school for an induction day before the summer holidays. Even so, I was a bit nervous.

As I entered the gates an older lad approached me.

'New here?' he enquired.

'Er… yes. How did you know?'

'Creases.'

'What?'

'Your trousers. Creases. Only new kids have creases. Don't worry, they'll soon disappear. Know where you're going?' he asked.

'Main hall. It's down that way, isn't it?' I checked.

'Yep.'

I walked on, lifting my knees artificially high in order to try to press the revealing creases out of my new school trousers. The exaggerated knee movement was complicated by the weight of the rucksack on my back and gave my forward movement something of the appearance of a caterpillar attempting to walk on its hindmost legs. In this rather ungainly fashion, I arrived at the hall where I was relieved to see one or two faces I recognised from my primary school.

Once everyone was seated Mrs Smoothing, the teacher-in-charge-of-helping-new-pupils-settle-in, welcomed us and then handed over to the Head for his 'welcoming talk'.

He rose to his feet and began. 'This school takes great pride in its academic, sporting and musical achievements. Our exam results last year were the best on record, more of our pupils play for county sports teams than ever before, and our school band has just returned from a summer tour of Europe. You have joined a successful school, and we expect every one of you to benefit from and contribute to its future success.

'We will expect politeness, punctuality and persistent effort at all times. Three Ps – Politeness, Punctuality, Persistent Effort. We believe that every pupil can deliver all the Ps, and if you don't' – he paused while he searched for a suitable punishment, before concluding somewhat unexpectedly – 'you should be put in a barrel and pushed off a cliff.'

Oh wow! I had still been trying to rub the creases out of my trousers, and consequently my attention had begun to wander. But the Head's last words grabbed it back with a start. Did he really say, 'If you don't eat all your peas, you will be put in a barrel and pushed off a cliff!'?

Mum had some pretty tough ways of getting me to eat my carrots, but this was a bit extreme. My mind raced back to the induction day before the summer holidays. I was sure there had been nothing about being tortured for failing to finish your vegetables, nor was it mentioned in the school prospectus – a grave omission (if you'll pardon the pun).

This was a deeply alarming turn of events (I'm allergic to peas) and the rest of the Head's talk was lost to my whirring mind.

How many peas would I be expected to eat? Maybe I could persuade a friend to eat them for me. Would that count? If not, then who exactly would put me in the barrel, and which cliff edge would I be pushed over? Surely they had to send a letter home first!

Some of Mum's last advice flooded back to my mind. 'Don't be afraid to ask questions,' she had said. 'Be polite,' she had said. So, as the Head drew his talk to a close, I ventured to put my hand in the air.

'Oh, a question. That's rather unusual. But go ahead, laddie. What would you like to know?' The Head beamed encouragingly at this unexpected display of interest in his speech.

'Please, Sir, I'm too young to die and I don't like peas. The doctor said they caused the rash on my bottom… but I'll have double carrots if that would be OK… but if it's not, then could it be a big barrel 'cause I get dizzy in small spaces, and please could I ring home to say goodbye to my gerbil first? Please, Sir.'

I later learned that Headteachers seldom lose control

10

of the entire new intake on their first day in school, but my question caused quite a stir among my fellow pupils. So much so, that I was removed in the custody of Mrs Smoothing to explain myself while the Head attempted to regain his composure in the hall.

Shame… I'd been looking forward to this day and it had all gone wrong already. Maybe going up to Big School wasn't quite as straightforward as I'd imagined!

The really important bit

Let's be honest: there is nothing at all in the Bible about the major challenge of going up to secondary school! However, there is a well-known story about God's special nation, Israel, facing the major challenge of crossing the River Jordan to live in the country of Canaan. Strange though it might seem, several of the things that God said to Israel at that point in their history make good advice for people going up to secondary school! Sound far-fetched? Read on.

1   The Lord said to Joshua, 'My servant Moses is dead' (Joshua 1:2).

Now this really was no surprise to Joshua! He had become Israel's new leader precisely because the famous leader Moses had recently died! Joshua knew that Moses was dead, so why does God point it out to him AGAIN? Maybe because Joshua had to realise that the old way of life had gone for good and there was no point in trying to go back to the way things were. Moses was dead and Joshua was in charge. There were new challenges ahead that required new leadership, new ideas, new ways of coping – just about new everything!

You may have enjoyed primary school. You may have liked your teacher, or your classroom, or the friends that you had there. But these have gone now. 'Your primary school is dead' (at least as far as you are concerned!) so don't expect things to be the same at secondary school. You are entering a new phase of your life, a chance to start again with a clean sheet. Make up your mind to make the most of it!

2 God said, 'I will always be with you; I will never abandon you' (Joshua 1:5).

This must have been a great encouragement to Joshua. He needed to know that he was not going into Canaan alone but that God was with him.

You may have many friends from primary school going up to secondary school at the same time, or you may be going alone. But remember this – the most important friend you could want is going to be there with you. Jesus will walk into school alongside you, and he will be just a prayer away all the time that you are there.

3 God said, 'Be determined and confident' (Joshua 1:6).

Or, to put it another way, 'There really is nothing to be afraid of, Joshua, so approach the future with a determination to get on with what you have to do.'

These words could have been written just for you. Secondary school may appear very big and threatening, but the teachers aren't really allowed to torture you (not without your parents' written permission anyway!). Be determined to take the opportunities that your new school gives you. If you didn't get on too well at primary school, be determined not to make the same mistakes again. If you had some friends who got you into trouble at primary school, be determined to choose your friends more carefully at your new school.

4 Make sure that you obey everything in God's law (Joshua 1:8).

The secret of Joshua's success in moving into Canaan wouldn't be the strength of his army but the strength of his commitment to God. There were times when he was tempted to do things his way, but whenever he did that he always got into big trouble. It was only when he obeyed God's way of doing things that his armies were successful.

In secondary school you will have lots of new pressures and opportunities. Sometimes you will be tempted by your friends to get involved in things that you know are wrong. Say 'No'. Put God's way first and, even if your friends think you're mad, don't be tempted to give up what you believe in.

5 Then Joshua ordered the leaders to tell the people to GET READY! (Joshua 1:10–11).

God is very practical. He WOULD be with his people. They DID need to be confident and committed. BUT that didn't mean that they shouldn't also make practical preparations for the task ahead.

God will be with you in school, but you could still take some practical steps to make sure that your first few days at secondary school are as easy as possible (see the 'Survival strategy' below).

6 Joshua sent two spies to go and explore the land of Canaan (Joshua 2:1).

It was important for the Israelites to know what was ahead of them, so Joshua sent some spies on an induction day to Canaan! They had a sneak preview of what it was like, then they came back to encourage the rest of the people that it wasn't so bad after all!

Every secondary school has special induction days for its new pupils. Don't miss yours. It will give you a tremendously helpful insight into your new school. You will probably meet your new form teacher, see your new classmates and classrooms, find the toilets and hundreds of other useful things. You will probably be given some information about the new school, but take a small notebook with you in case you spy out anything for yourself you particularly want to remember.

Survival strategy!

1 Make full use of your induction day. Gather as much information as you can.

2 If you're worried about anything, ask your parents or, when you get to school, your form teacher or tutor. They will be only too pleased to help.

Your tutor is an important person in helping you to settle in well. If you have ANY questions or problems ('Where are the nearest toilets to the gym?' 'I've forgotten my dinner money. What do I do?' 'Where is Room T6 for technology?'), don't be frightened to ask your tutor or any other teacher.

3   At your primary school you were among the biggest pupils. In your new school, you will be one of the smallest and you will have to be prepared for your new status in life! However, just because you are one of the youngest and smallest, it doesn't mean that anyone else has the right to pick on you. So if anyone does try it, tell your tutor or another teacher straight away. If it happens again and you're worried, make sure you tell someone at home too.

4   You may have to travel a lot further to your new school. If possible, do a dummy run before the first day to work out the best route and how long it will take.

5   The change of school will probably leave you feeling very tired at first. Be ready to have a few early nights before term starts and during the first couple of weeks.

6   Your new school may seem huge. The school will probably provide you with a map so that you can find your way around. But if you get lost, don't panic. Just ask for advice. Teachers EXPECT some new pupils to get lost in the first couple of days, so don't worry if you arrive late for a lesson because you couldn't find the room!

7   Most (but not all) secondary schools have a school uniform and your parents may well have spent a lot of money buying it, along with new sports kit, stationery items and so on. Make sure your name is on EVERYTHING. If you lose anything, first check the place where you last remember having it and then check the school office (or wherever the lost property is collected).

8   If some of your friends from primary school are going up to the same new school, arrange to meet up and travel together (or at least meet up at the school gates) for the first day. You will soon get used to your new surroundings, but on Day 1 you may well appreciate having your friends with you.

9   Don't leave valuables (including trainers and coats) lying around anywhere. Sadly, things do get stolen in secondary schools, so keep a careful eye on your stuff. If lockers are provided, make sure you get one and keep your possessions safe. (Keep the key on a piece of string around your neck, not in your pocket or pencil case!)

10 Be very careful about making new friends. Every class has its share of people whose sole aim is to mess about and do as little work as humanly possible! The Bible says that 'Bad companions ruin good character' (1 Corinthians 15:33), so don't allow your good character to be ruined by falling in with 'bad companions'!

11 Get hold of a copy of *It's Your Move!*, published by Scripture Union (ISBN 9781844275090). It's packed with great advice about moving up to secondary school, including an A-Z survival guide, plus real-life stories from students, and pages for collecting friends' autographs. You can buy it at Christian bookshops, or online at www.scriptureunion.org.uk/publishing, or by calling Mail Order direct on 08450 706 006.

Think about it

1 In the space below, write down the thing that most concerns you about going up to secondary school. Pray about it and find the right moment to talk to your mum or dad or the person who cares for you, about it.

2 Think of any of your friends who might be worried about going up to secondary school. Pray for them and offer to go into your new school together on the first day.

With friends like those

(Following God or following the crowd)

Jayzee, Dude D and the Mattmeister. The three names brought a lump to my throat, a tear to my eye and the sort of feeling to my stomach that I'd once had after eating a double cheeseburger and chips on a particularly rough sea crossing.

Jayzee (really James), Dude D (David) and the Mattmeister (Matthew) – the self-appointed hard men of Year 8. Their chosen purpose in life – to protect the whole class from outbreaks of Nerdish Behaviour, Naff Clothing and Stoopid Sayings.

If, for example, you're foolish enough to wear regulation school uniform, you're guilty of breaking the Naff Clothing rule and immediately become the target for comments like, 'Mummy dress you this morning, did she?'; if you don't have the latest mobile phone package then you're certainly demonstrating Nerdish Behaviour and get immediately expelled from the 'in crowd'. As for Stoopid Sayings, the rules are simple:

1 Never pronounce the H at the beginning of words.
2 Never pronounce D or T at the end of words.
3 Occasionally miss D's or T's from the middle of words.
4 Wherever possible slur two or more words together.

5 Learn to use words that are meaningless to adults.
6 Never say 'please', 'thank you' or 'sorry'.
7 Swear as often as you can.

By the straightforward application of these rules you could say things like:

'Arsalrye, byate istree.'

(Translated: 'Art is all right, but I hate history.')

or

'See the foodie laznye? Brill wunni.'

('Did you see the football last night? It was brilliant, wasn't it?')

Jayzee, Dude D and the Mattmeister...
the self-appointed hard men of Year 8.

Anyway, the reason for my special fear of facing the terrible trio this morning was founded on three facts. Firstly my trainer socks were in the wash, and I'd lost my trainers. I was therefore forced to resort to standard regulation school footwear – grey socks and boring ordinary shoes. Naff Clothing – guilty!

Secondly, I'd been to a church youth group meeting last night and not watched one minute of TV. Nerdish Behaviour – guilty!

Thirdly, after our maths lesson yesterday I'd made the mistake of being overheard saying, 'I'm really sorry for not finishing my homework, Sir,' to Mr Kent, the maths teacher. Of course I should have said, 'Cawuz sikoni wunnee?' ('The cat was sick on it wasn't he?') which would have been a lie but far less Stoopid – and possibly less Nerdish as well! Stoopid Sayings – guilty!

So there I was, totally guilty and with no way out. Or was there? Maybe there was. I quickly ripped off my school tie and stuffed it in my bag. With my top shirt-button undone, my shoe laces trailing and my shirt hanging outside of my trousers, I might just look scruffy enough to have a bit of 'cred' in the all-searching eyes of Jayzee, Dude D and the Mattmeister. Mum wouldn't approve of course, but she wouldn't know and I could always smarten myself up a bit before facing Mr Barnes, my class tutor. Phew, Naff Clothing crisis solved!

Nerdish Behaviour was easier; after all, no one knew that I'd been to a church youth group last night. If I told a few well-placed lies (I call them half-truths to make myself feel better) no one need be any the wiser. OK, I was at home drinking Coke and watching the James

Bond film just like everybody else.

But what to do about the allegations of Stoopid Sayings? After all, there were eye-witnesses (or rather, ear-witnesses) to my apologies to Mr Kent. A possible way out of my dilemma was to deny that I'd meant it and to laugh at Mr Kent for being so easily taken in by my 'sincere' apology. Yes, in fact, if I was rude enough about Mr Kent and if I threw in a few swear words, Jayzee, Dude D and the Mattmeister might be so impressed they'd completely forget about my original Stoopid Saying!

The really important bit

It can be hard to do what's right at school when your friends (never mind your enemies) expect you to do something else. The pressure to do what they expect and to fit in with their way of doing things is *enormous*. To try to do something which is different from what everyone else is doing can make you the object of cruel comments or ridicule. It's sometimes far easier to blend in with what's going on, and give up what you know to be right, in order to be accepted by the 'in crowd'. Right?

The trouble is that after you've sworn, lied, deceived your parents, told the dirty joke – or whatever – you feel guilty and ashamed. You know you've let God down and you're not sure what to do to put it right.

Well firstly, if you have failed, don't give up! You may have lost that particular battle to do what's right, but you haven't lost the entire war – that goes on for the rest of your life!

Have you ever read the bit in the Bible where Peter, one of Jesus' best friends, is watching Jesus after he has been arrested? In the courtyard where Peter is sitting there's a whole lot of people and some of them recognise that Peter is a friend of Jesus. Now, Jesus was becoming pretty unpopular at that time and Peter knew that if he was identified as a friend of Jesus, he'd become pretty unpopular too. So he had to think – fast. His solution was simple: lie.

'Peter was sitting outside in the courtyard when one of the High Priest's servant-girls came to him and said, "You, too, were with Jesus of Galilee." But he denied it in front of them all. "I don't know what you are talking about," he answered … Another servant-girl saw him and said to the men there, "He was with Jesus of Nazareth." Again Peter denied it and answered, "I swear that I don't know that man!"' (Matthew 26:69–72)

Peter recovered from that failure: although he let Jesus down, Jesus gave him a starring role in the early church. So a few mistakes don't mean it's all over!

Survival strategy!

1   Of course it's not always true that your friends will only be doing bad things – most of the time many of your friends will be fun to be with and fit in with. But because you're trying to live your life to please Jesus and your non-Christian friends are not, there will be times when you'll need to be prepared to be different.

You see, you don't have to allow other people to run your life. You don't HAVE TO wear the sort of clothes that they wear, listen to the music that they listen to, go to the places that they go, watch the things that they watch, say the things that they say etc! As a Christian you have chosen Jesus to be the Lord of your life. That means that he's the boss – and that makes a lot of sense, because he invented life, so he knows what advice to give you to make YOUR life as good as possible. The Jayzee's, Dude D's and the Mattmeister's of this world may have their own ideas on life, but they are not God, so it doesn't make much sense following them and their way of doing things if it contradicts what God says.

Sometimes life gives you a basic choice; please your friends or please God. The decision is yours.

---

2   Make sure that you have some friendships with other Christians in your school. Then if the going gets a bit tough with your non-Christian friends, you won't be on your own. You can turn to your Christian friends for support and encouragement. You could even pray together about the situation!

---

3   Get your faith in God out into the open. It's always a mistake to hide what you believe, hoping that sometime in the future you'll find it easier to tell your friends that you go to church, believe in God, pray and read the Bible. It doesn't get easier – in fact, it gets harder the longer you leave it.

4   Maybe some of your 'friends' will laugh at you because you go to church. That's only because they don't understand who God really is, and what following him is really all about.

The thing is, if they really are FRIENDS, they won't laugh at you, but will accept the fact that you believe something different to them. Friends who don't allow you to be yourself with them, but want you to be someone that you are not, are really not very good friends at all; you're probably better off without them!

Think about it

1 In the space below, write down the names of your three best friends at school. Write next to each name what it is that you like about that person.

2 Still thinking of your three best friends, is there anything about your friendship with them that causes you to feel uncomfortable? (For example, do they expect you to join in with things that you know upset God? Do they swear? etc.) Pray that God will give you the strength to stand up for what you know to be right and to be a good influence on your friends.

3 In the space below write down one thing that you want to do differently in your friendships at school as a result of reading this chapter.

A testing time

(Coping with feeling a failure)

Some poor misguided individual once said that 'school days are the happiest days of your life.' Well, it's true enough that some school days are happy (for example, the school day before half-term holidays, the school day before Christmas holidays, the school day the boiler blew up and we all got sent home early etc, etc!). But whoever it was that made that claim obviously did not have a school day on which he was expected to use MY brain to do one of Mr Kent's maths tests! Pitting my brain against Mr Kent's maths test did not make me happy. Fed-up: yes. Depressed: yes. Happy: no.

Maths tests are OK provided that
(a) you can make yourself see the point in doing them
(b) you can get your brain cells around the answer
(c) you've done at least some work in the last two weeks' maths lessons.

To be honest, I had problems on all three counts. With regard to point (c), I had been a teensy bit lazy in the last few maths lessons, not having worked on the set tasks with much enthusiasm at all. This was partly due to the fact that I didn't really understand what I was supposed to be doing and partly because I had a very intricate felt-pen and biro decoration to complete on my pencil case

25

(which obviously took priority over maths work).

As for point (b), I couldn't even get my brain cells around the questions, never mind the answers. I always try to read the question calmly at first, because I hope that if I read them slowly enough the words will, in some miraculous way, make sense to me. But then with an ever-deepening sinking feeling inside, I realise that I am bound for failure once again. Achieving a maths mark in double figures (all tests are marked out of 50) was about as likely as Iceland winning the Eurovision song contest or Jackie Chan having the lead role in a slushy romantic comedy!

And so to point (a). Some maths work will, I am sure, be very helpful in later life; I just wish we could get to that bit soon! So many of the problems that we have to solve just have nothing at all to do with real life. Take, for example, the following:

PROBLEM

Your mum goes to Tesco with £50.00 in her purse. She spends £27.87 and leaves the store. On her way home she remembers that she forgot to get any pet food so she returns to the shop to buy some. She buys three tins of dog food at 66p each and a box of Miaow Krunchies at £1.16. You normally receive £5.00 a week pocket money. When your mum finally returns from shopping, how many weeks' pocket money does she have in her purse?

Now I have difficulties with this type of problem, because
(a) my dad does the shopping on his way home from

work on a Friday, so my mum never goes to the supermarket

(b) Mum never has more than £10.00 in her purse because she always pays for everything by debit card

(c) there is no Tesco supermarket in our town

(d) our weekly shopping bill is more like £60.00 than £27.87

(e) we don't have a dog and our cat died last week

(f) and as if I get £5.00 pocket money a week!

I'm sure that you can see the reasons for the brain-strain caused by trying to get to grips with this sort of puzzle. Here's another example:

PROBLEM

Each time you fill the bath, the water flows in at the rate of 15 litres per minute through the cold tap and 12 litres per minute through the hot tap (when they are fully turned on). The water flows out through the plug hole at the rate of 8 litres per minute and the bath holds 500 litres before it overflows. It you were filling the bath with both taps on and the plug out, how many minutes would it be before the bath overflowed?

Now doubtless to some people this is an everyday situation and so they have no problems in tackling it as a mathematical exercise. However I must, once again, admit that I have certain problems with applying my brain to this situation.

My problems may be explained thus

(a) I always have showers so have little experience of bath taps

(b) If I WERE to take a bath, I wouldn't turn both taps fully on since this is bound to result in a freezing cold bath

(c) Even if I DID turn both taps fully on, I would not attempt to fill my bath with the plug out

(d) Even if I DID turn both taps fully on and DID leave

...how many minutes before the bath overflowed?

the plug out, I would not allow the bath to get anywhere near overflowing because my mum would beat me around the head with the back-scrubber!

Although I may be seeming to make light of my brain's struggles, there is a serious side to it. You see, when your brain doesn't manage to do what teachers want it to, the world can begin to seem an unhappy place. So-called 'friends' start to make fun of you (Question: 'What's the difference between David's brain and a dustbin?' Answer: 'At least a dustbin's got rubbish in it'), teachers try to 'encourage' you ('You'll just have to stay in at break time to do it all again') and parents begin to give up on you becoming the little genius that they always hoped you'd turn out to be!

To be honest I'm beginning to get fed up with being so useless and just wish that 'Failure' wasn't my middle name. Why couldn't I have been born to be successful and brainy?

The really important bit

Well, it all depends on what you mean by words like 'successful', 'useless' and 'failure'. You may have been conned into believing that successful human beings are the ones with loads of brains and loads of friends, but the truth is different!

Some of the people who became the greatest successes in the Bible were the weediest failures in the eyes of other people at the time. Take Gideon, for example. He was hiding from his enemies when God sent an angel to talk to him. Gideon describes himself as a member of the weakest group in his tribe and as 'the least important member' of his family! In other words Gideon was the pits in his own eyes – a coward and an unimportant member of an unimpressive family! Poor Gideon.

But just listen to how God sees him. God says to this jelly-heap of a man, 'The LORD is with you, brave and mighty man!' (Judges 6:12) Gideon probably wondered who God was speaking to!

You see, the truth is that God does not see ANY human being as unimportant, worthless or useless – not even a Gideon or a YOU! No matter what other people may say, do or think, and no matter what you may even have begun to believe yourself, there are two strong reasons why God thinks you're an OK person.

Firstly, you can know that you are an OK person because you are the most fantastically designed, most wonderfully advanced and most incredibly complicated part of God's world! Your body – even if it can't do Mr Kent's maths tests or win the high jump – remains something that modern science cannot copy. No robots or computers anywhere in the world can imitate the complex functions of your human body. So when God looks at you, he doesn't see FAILURE stamped across your face, because you (and every other human being) are the best thing that he ever created. He looks at you with pride, pleasure and admiration simply because you are part of the human race – that's enough.

John wrote these words: 'God loved the world so much that he gave his only Son, so that everyone who believes in him may not die but have eternal life' (John 3:16). He did NOT write these words: 'God loved the brainy people and attractive people in the world so much that he gave his only Son, so that anyone with 8 GCSEs, 3 A Levels and loads of friends may not die but have eternal life!'

In fact Jesus made it his business to befriend people who everyone else called failures. He went out of his way to spend time with unpopular, even hated people – like Zacchaeus. (Check out the chapter on Loving the Jesus way.) Surely he's got loads of time for people who struggle at maths, sport, spelling etc?

The second reason why God does not give up on you as a hopeless case is because he can see the future. He knows that you are an extremely useful human being and there are things that need doing in the world that you are just the person to do.

Just like God saw that Gideon (El Wimpo) was the man to defeat the armies of the Midianites (read about it in Judges 6–8): he saw that the murderer Moses was just the man to free his people Israel from the grip of slavery in Egypt. Just as Jesus chose the unpredictable, speak-now-think-later Peter as a disciple, and called him 'a rock', God chose the nervous, young, inexperienced Jeremiah to preach strong sermons to Israel and the surrounding countries. God seems to get a real kick out of choosing people who think that they are useless, or who others think are useless, and using them for something important and useful.

So even though today, every one of them would probably have been chosen as the Weakest Link, and immediately asked to leave the stage with a suitably stony stare, God chose Gideon to be a military hero, Moses to be a great leader, Peter to be a rock-like dependable person, and Jeremiah to be a powerful preacher.

Now believe this – you are not the Weakest Link, either! Whatever the state of your test results, God can make your life useful and successful IF you are willing to do what he asks you to.

Survival strategy!

1   Refuse to believe any opinion about yourself EXCEPT God's opinion – that as a human being you are valuable, successful and useful.

2   If you find certain aspects of school work difficult, don't just give up; ask your teachers why they think you find it hard, and how you can begin to cope a bit better.

3   Make your aim each day to do your best, NOT to get full marks or be top of the class. If your aim each day is to do your best, then every day can be a success because you can always go home knowing that you HAVE done your best (whatever marks you get). If your aim is to be cleverest, fastest, neatest – or whatever – you will frequently be disappointed when others beat you.

4   Look out for the things that you CAN do at school, and develop those as much as possible. God has made everybody good at different things, so try to discover what it is that God has given you the ability to do, and try to do it as well as possible. Enjoy what you can do

and don't get too worried about what you can't.

5 Do all that you can to encourage other people in your class who are struggling with certain subjects and activities. Never mock other people who find the work difficult (you know how much you hate being laughed at). Congratulate them for the things that they are good at.

Think about it

1 In the space below write the name of someone in your class who struggles with the work and who you could try to encourage.

2 Think about any areas of difficulty which you experience with your school work. Are you doing your best at it? If so, you're succeeding!

Teachers!

(Teachers are people too – honest!)

The trouble with teachers is that they are always right
– even when they're wrong! Take 'Boggers' for example.
(Actually 'Boggers' is really called Mr Jones, but his hair
stands up like the bristles on a bog... er... toilet brush,
hence his nickname.)

'Boggers' takes us for science and he is, by common
agreement, a bit of a wimp – at least he is on some days.
On other occasions he acts like a cross between the
Hulk, Hitler and Albert Einstein! But that's precisely
the problem – you never know where you stand with
him. One lesson he can be really soft and anyone could
get away with murder (well, almost) and the next lesson
he goes all strict on you and starts giving out lines and
detentions like they are past their sell-by date.

Of course 'Boggers' isn't the only teacher with his own
funny little ways; all teachers take a bit of getting used to.
In fact that's another problem with teachers – they're all
different. There's the 'line-up-outside-the-door-and-you-
can't-come-in-until-you're-quiet' sort, and there's the
'if-you-get-there-before-me-go-in-and-get-on-with-some-
thing' sort. There's the 'OK-let's-discuss-this-together'
sort, and the 'don't-answer-back-I'm-in-charge-here' sort.
Then again there's the 'right-I-warned-you-off-to-the-
Head's-study' sort, and the 'I'll-pretend-I-didn't-hear-
that' sort. Do you get the picture? Worst of all is when,

for no good reason, a teacher goes all heavy-duty on you – like last week in music.

Mrs Glen is pretty well-liked, for a teacher. She always tries to make the lesson interesting and we all really like it when we work in groups with percussion instruments, composing music. Last Thursday was supposed to be a practical lesson, but when we got there Mrs Glen told us that we'd have to carry on with our writing topic. Apparently there was an exam in the hall next door to the music room and we had to be quiet. Well, we were really disappointed, and a few of us said so.

...I emerge with a handful of dismembered glockenspiel bars.

As a protest some people never really made any attempt to get on with their writing project but just sat there and chatted to each other. After about ten minutes Mr Morris, the violin teacher who visits the school, came in and wanted a word with Mrs Glen. She went outside to talk to him, threatening all sorts of terrible punishments for anyone who misbehaved in her absence. The minute the door closed behind her, chaos broke out. The precise sequence of events went like this:

1 James falls off his chair (accidentally!) and knocks Anya's desk.
2 Anya (normally a quiet girl) thumps James because he has knocked her and spoilt her drawing of a tuba.
3 James pushes Anya and she falls over onto the cake that Sophie has just baked in home economics.
4 Andy (Sophie's twin brother) and Ryan (who fancies Anya) jump on James (who fancies himself) to the accompaniment of loud cheering from everyone else.
5 The glockenspiel on Mrs Glen's desk gets knocked over, its tuned bars clattering to the ground like heavy-metal confetti.
6 I crawl under her desk to pick up all the bits.
7 Mrs Glen re-enters the room.
8 Everyone else sits down and resumes work as though nothing had happened.
9 I emerge from under her desk with a handful of dismembered glockenspiel bars.

Now, I ask you; what would you have thought? Well, it will surprise you to know that Mrs Glen thought I, me, myself, personally had been up to no good. What is more, she said so – in no uncertain terms. Which proves my point about teachers; even the best of them can go completely over the top, for no reason whatsoever. Well, I can't see a reason, can you?!

The really important bit

It may be hard to believe this, but every single teacher is a human being! They don't sleep in the staff room at night, plugged in to the power supply like Rechargeable Humanoid Education Machines. They go home, eat, sleep and watch TV like everyone else. What's more, they have feelings! They can be happy and cheerful but they can also get fed up, frustrated, angry, disappointed and hurt inside – just like real people. What's more, God loves them just as much as he loves you, and he wants YOU to show them his love.

Hang on a minute; love teachers?! NO – don't shut the book, read on!

You see, God is concerned about every human being and he wants his followers to share that concern. In fact – and this is going to blow your socks off if you've never thought about it before – God works out how much we love him by the way we treat other people (including teachers). Get your brain cells around these Bible verses:

'If you laugh at poor people [or teachers], you insult the God who made them' (Proverbs 17:5).

'If someone says he loves God, but hates his brother

[or teacher], he is a liar. For he cannot love God, whom he has not seen, if he does not love his brother [or teacher], whom he has seen. The command that Christ has given us is this: whoever loves God must love his brother [teacher] also' (1 John 4:20–21).

You see, every single human being is a bit like a photocopy of God. The Bible says that humans (you, me and teachers!) are made to be like God. It's true that all of us human beings manage to cover up our God-likeness with all sorts of unkind and bad behaviour. Maybe we are like a photocopy of God that got a bit crumpled and smudged as it came out of the machine so that his image in us has got a bit spoilt, but that doesn't alter the fact that every person has something of God about them. Therefore, when we laugh at other people, we laugh at the image of God in them; when we are rude to them, we are rude to the image of God in them; when we refuse to help them, we refuse to help the image of God in them. Of course the opposite is also true. When we help them, God sees it as helping him; when we are kind to them, God counts it as a kindness done to him, and so on. Jesus made all this very plain in the story about the sheep and the goats. (Read it for yourself in Matthew 25:31–46.)

So what has all this got to say to us about 'Boggers', Mrs Glen and all teachers (good and bad) everywhere? Well, it means that whatever other people's attitude to teachers may be, Christians are expected to love them, because however successfully they manage to hide it, all teachers are human – designed by God to carry his likeness. To put it even more plainly (with apologies to John!)…

If someone says he loves God, but hates 'Boggers', he is a liar. For he cannot love God, whom he has not seen, if he does not love 'Boggers', whom he has seen. The command that Christ has given us is this: whoever loves God must love 'Boggers' also!

Of course this is easy to say but difficult to do. How do you love teachers? Offer to do all their marking for them? Clean their Citroen 2CV at break? Well maybe not! Here, to get you started, are some ideas...

Survival strategy!

1   Remember why you are going to try to love teachers. Not to gain extra marks in the test and certainly not to impress your friends! They probably won't see things in the same way as you do, because you're trying to do what God wants and your friends may not be. But God sees what you're doing, understands why you're doing it and is really chuffed to bits when you try to do what he wants.

2   Try to see things from your teachers' point of view. For example, in the story above, Mrs Glen may have jumped to the wrong conclusion, but if you were Mrs Glen how would YOU feel if you were tired, your lesson had been disrupted by exams in the hall next door, several people in the class were being awkward, you got interrupted by an unhappy violin teacher moaning about his pupils not turning up on time and then you re-enter your classroom to find someone crawling under your desk with a handful of expensive musical instrument?! Let's be honest and admit that any one of us would have

found our patience being stretched a bit thin!

3 Try never to do or say anything to a teacher (or about a teacher) that you would not like done or said to you. Why should they put up with behaviour from you, that you yourself would find hurtful?

4 Teachers make mistakes (because they are human!). Don't bear grudges against them and don't keep on repeating their mistakes to others so that you can all have a really good laugh at their expense.

5 Have the courage to own up to your mistakes and to say sorry when you're responsible for any bad behaviour.

6 Pray for your teachers.

7 If you've enjoyed a particular lesson or activity it would encourage your teacher to get a 'thank you' occasionally. Try and give out one 'thank you' a day; it won't hurt too much, I promise!

Think about it

1 In this space write in your own words one thing that you've learnt about how to relate to teachers.

2   In this space write one thing that you intend to do to improve your relationships with teachers.

3   In this space write the name of one teacher who you find difficult to get on with and who you could begin to pray for.

Pick on someone your own size

(Being bullied)

The thing that I like best about Sports Day is the night before it.

On the night before Sports Day I am the school's champion athlete. I beat the school's fastest runner in the 100 metres sprint, breaking the finishing tape just before the other runners manage to leave their starting blocks; I smash the school long jump record by 15 metres (give or take a metre) and I hurl the discus so far that Miss Harrison, the teacher in charge of the event, has to get her battered Mini from the car park to retrieve it for the next competitor (who manages a measly 25 cm). The teachers are forced to cancel the 800 metres when the other competitors all withdraw rather than be humiliated by being beaten by me. And my mum is moved to tears of joy and pride as I win the 43,100 metres relay race on my own. At the end of the afternoon's events the Head makes an emotional speech praising my athleticism, my versatility, my stamina and my humility as he kneels at my feet to present me with the 'School's Outstanding Sportsperson of the Decade' award. Later, at home, my dad puts up another five shelves in my bedroom to display the trophies that have just been delivered by a big armoured truck.

That, as I said, all happens (in my imagination, of course) on the night before Sports Day. On the actual day itself the reality is, well, sort of different.

To start with I must admit that I'm not actually very fit. I can't really understand that, since I exercise regularly (I walk to the sweet shop at least twice a day) and I eat loads of fitness foods (like Mars bars and Diet Coke for instance). Anyway, since I don't seem to be the owner of a super-fit body I thought it best this year to enter an event that required the minimum of movement.

Hurling my body through the air in the jumps didn't seem too appealing, nor did attempting to sprint, run or hurdle my way into the record books: but how about throwing something? Yes, surely the shot-put would be the ideal event for an athlete such as me. All you have to do is stand still, then in a sudden, short burst of activity you chuck this sort of cannon-ball-like object as far as you can. If you can also grunt loudly as you release the shot, this gives the impression to watching parents that you are putting huge amounts of effort into the event. This always goes down well and may even result in a congratulatory Mars bar whether you win (unlikely) or lose (strong possibility).

Having entered for the shot-put and having practised by throwing half bricks at our next-door neighbour's cat (which happily stayed out of range of the missiles whilst becoming increasingly terrified by my ever-improving grunts), I arrived at school feeling pretty confident. Life took a sudden and terrible turn for the worse, however, when I read the list of competitors that I was to throw against. There were just three names in the shot-put column: Darren White's, James Kirkby's and mine. Darren White posed no threat since he was about as athletic as me, but James Kirkby (better known as 'Jayzee') was another matter.

Jayzee's one of those people who gets his own way. One of those people that you don't argue with (not twice anyway). Jayzee isn't into polite conversation or reasonable discussion in any big way. He's more into hitting people, threatening people or preferably both. He is, in some ways, a sort of humanoid Winnie the Pooh (the bear with very little brain) without any of Pooh's more lovable characteristics – although no one in their right mind would tell him so! His shortcomings in the world of study and his equally dismal record of sporting achievements do nothing to diminish his desire to perfect his skills of aggression and nastiness. And now, my problem was how to compete against Jayzee in that afternoon's shot-put competition. If I pulled out he would probably do me over for being a chicken, but if I competed and beat him (unlikely but not impossible)... well, I might as well have booked my hospital bed there and then. The only way to keep the peace (and both legs) was to compete, grunt like a hero but throw like a twit.

We were allowed two throws each. Darren threw first – a 'no throw'. I was next. I gave it all I had and, grunting loudly enough to raise the dead, I achieved 3 metres 25 cm.

Jayzee laughed and 'accidentally' trod on my foot as he made his way to take his first throw. He steadied himself in the concrete throwing circle, spun round in a professional shot-putting style and threw the shot 3 metres 78 cm. Phew, thank goodness for that! So far so good; now all I had to do was to muck up my second throw and Jayzee would be the winner.

Darren went first again and achieved 3 metres 50 cm this time, which drew encouraging but sympathic comments from his watching friends. I picked up the shot, got my balance and hurled the shot. I must have underestimated the benefit of my practise with the neighbour's cat, since my attempt seemed to sail on and on before it thudded to the ground. In actual fact it was only 3 metres 90 cm but what had I done? I told myself not to panic; to stay cool. Surely Jayzee could better that; after all, his first attempt had nearly got him that far.

He gave me a hard stare, which said all that I needed to know about my fate if he failed to beat me. Picking up the shot he crouched low at the back of the throwing circle – he was obviously going to put every last gram of effort into preserving his reputation. He began to move, spinning quickly on the ball of his right foot. Surely this was to be the winning throw, but, oh disaster, gloom and stress, it wasn't. Halfway through his super-human effort his foot slipped and in mid-launch he came down in an uncoordinated heap, just outside the throwing circle. The shot slipped from his grasp and nearly flattened the Head's wife, who was standing at a safe distance (or so she thought) behind the thrower.

Actually, the shot didn't flatten her, but Jayzee's choice of language did. I'd heard most of the words that Jayzee used to express his feelings at his misfortune; the Head's wife hadn't, apparently, since Jayzee was immediately dragged off to the Head's office to 'explain himself'.

Now don't ask me why, but ever since that fateful day Jayzee hasn't liked me much. Whenever we pass

The shot slipped from his grasp and nearly flattened the Head's wife.

in the corridor he aims a kick at me or tries to take my bag or… well, I'm sure you can imagine the situation. Trouble is it might have started as a bit of a joke but it's no joke now – not for me anyway. The prospect of doing battle with Jayzee every day is getting more and more depressing. In fact the other day I just couldn't face yet another day of taunts, kicks and bag-snatching so I skived off school. I told my mum that I had a headache so she let me stay at home. I can't keep on doing that though, can I, so what can I do?

The really important bit

If you are being bullied at the moment, or have been bullied, you'll know how completely hurtful and upsetting it can be. Daily facing threats (and worse) from people who think they can get away with anything, just because they are physically stronger than you, is a miserable way to live. It may be comforting for you to know that God understands EXACTLY how you feel. You see, God has been bullied!

God experienced all the struggles of real life as a human when Jesus (the man who was God) lived on earth 2,000 years ago. OK so there were no school bullies of the Jayzee variety, but there were plenty of other sorts about! People with power and authority who didn't like the things that Jesus said and did, and who tried to threaten him or get him beaten up. Eventually they murdered him because they disliked him so much.

One of the biggest bullies at the time was the king, Herod. He wanted his own way and didn't care how he got it. There are three important things to learn about bullies from the Bible's description of Herod.

In Mark 6:14–29, you can read the tragic story of Herod ordering the execution of Jesus' cousin, John the Baptist. Herod had arrested John because John kept reminding Herod of how wrong he had been to marry Herodias, who was already married to Herod's brother Philip. Now you may have noticed that bullies don't like having their faults pointed out to them, and so Herod had John locked up in prison. However, Herod did not want to kill John, because, the Bible tells us, '[He] was afraid of John because he knew that John was a good and holy man' (Mark 6:20). Herod couldn't help but respect John, even as he picked on him. *Bullies are often confused by people who don't fight back but who continue to do what is right.*

There was this guy called Rick, who was learning bricklaying at a local college. When the other students discovered that he was a Christian they picked on him all the time, frequently ruining his work. He refused to fight back and just kept on doing his best (even though he often went home upset). The bullying got worse and worse until eventually one day the leader of the gang came to him and apologised for being so mean! He explained that he had never met anyone before who didn't fight back. He didn't know how to cope with someone who was nice to him all the time because all the other people that he knew best (including his parents) had always been unkind to him.

Back to Herod, and the second thing to learn from him about bullies. As I've just said, Herod didn't intend to kill John the Baptist but his wife, Herodias, did. She hated John, and when Herod rashly promised Herodias' daughter anything she wanted, Herodias made her daughter ask for the head of John the Baptist. Herod, even then, didn't have to do it. He could have saved John, but because he didn't want to look soft in front of all the important people who'd heard him promise Herodias' daughter whatever she wanted, Herod killed John as requested.

Herod and all bullies everywhere are basically very weak people who get tough partly to try to hide their

weakness. The sort of weakness that I'm talking about isn't physical weakness but a weakness of their personality. They're often not very confident (however they may appear) and always want to impress their friends by doing nasty stuff, so that they feel wanted and accepted by the 'in crowd' – just like Herod. Being nasty is often the only thing they're good at, and so being successful at it makes them feel important. Sad, isn't it, when a human being can only feel good about themselves by being nasty to other people?

The third thing that the Bible teaches us about bullies is how to treat them. Herod's still at it, but this time he's feeling worried because so many people keep telling him how wonderful this Jesus person is. Bullies like to be Number One and the thought that someone else might be muscling in on his top-spot gets Herod in a bit of a strop. He responds like a true bully – by issuing threats.

'... some Pharisees came to Jesus and said to him, "You must get out of here and go somewhere else, because Herod wants to kill you."' (Luke 13:31).

Now Jesus knew that Herod had killed John and that therefore this might be no empty threat. But this is how Jesus responds:

'"Go and tell that fox: 'I am driving out demons and performing cures today and tomorrow, and on the third day I shall finish my work.'"' (Luke 13:32).

In other words: 'Go chase yourself, Herod. I'm going to keep doing what's right and no threats from you are going to stop me!' Although this route is tough, it's the only way to stop the bully. *If you give in to bullying and threats, then the bully wins and 'Wrong'*

has defeated 'Right'. Maybe at this point we ought to get on to a...

Survival strategy!

1 Whatever may have been threatened or done, don't give in to the bully, and don't keep whatever has happened to yourself. Tell a trusted friend – preferably an adult – and ask them for advice about what to do.

2 If hurtful things have been said to you or about you, don't let your mind keep going over and over them. Again, explain what's been said to a close friend and keep reminding yourself that in God's eyes you are a successful, important and useful person. (See chapter 3 – 'A testing time'.)

3 If things get really bad you MUST tell your parent(s) and one of your teachers. If any of your friends know what's been happening, take them with you.

4 Do everything that YOU can to avoid making matters worse. 'Do everything possible on your part to live in peace with everybody' (Romans 12:18). Don't deliberately stir up trouble.

5 Pray for the person who's picking on you. Ask God to use you to change that person for the better. And 'Ask God to bless those who persecute you – yes, ask him to bless, not to curse' (Romans 12:14). This is a really hard thing to do, but you need to give it a go.

6 'If someone has done you wrong, do not repay him with a wrong. Try to do what everyone considers to be good' (Romans 12:17). As we've already seen, the average bully can't cope with people who don't fight or answer back.

7 Walking away from a potentially ugly situation is not failure. Jesus did it (Luke 4:28–30) so it must make sense!

Think about it

1 In the space below write in your own words one thing you've learned which has helped you understand bullies better.

2 Write the names of anyone who you know is a bully or anyone who is being bullied. How can you help them?

Damnation Dominic

(Telling others about Jesus)

School yards are supposed to be safe places, and in general I suppose that they are. In my experience very few genuine disasters ever happen in the school yard. For example:

1 I have never seen anyone eaten by crocodiles.
2 I have never seen anyone flattened by a run-away horse and cart.
3 I have never seen anyone drown in a lake of boiling marmalade and...
4 I have never seen anyone fall down a disused mine shaft.

I could go on, but this is probably enough to prove my point – school yards are pretty safe. However, this safety is sometimes a fairly flimsy thing.

It is true that the perils of the average school yard are a bit different to those listed above, but none the less, perils there are! Here is my 'List of Potential Yard Perils':

1 Small pupils attempting to run between the legs of larger pupils playing football.
2 Larger pupils attempting to step over smaller pupils playing football.

3 Large pupils playing netball with smaller pupils (as opposed to with a ball).

4 Jayzee, Dude D and the Mattmeister. (See the second chapter, 'With friends like those'!)

5 Playing 'catch' with crisp bags full of water.

6 Opening the can of Coke that has been rattling around in your school bag all morning.

   Health warning! Perils 5 and 6 are especially dangerous if performed too near the member of staff on duty.

7 'Damnation Dominic'.

I reckon that you can all understand Perils 1–6 because they (or something very like them) are pretty common to all school yards. However, Peril number 7 may need some explanation because it is possible that you have never met a 'Damnation Dominic'.

'Damnation Dominic' is not strictly speaking a 'Peril', he is a person of the large, Year 12 variety. He is also a Christian and a member of the school Christian Union (room 19 – Friday lunch-time). Now 'Damnation Dominic' is not one of your wimpy-never-let-anyone-know-that-you-go-to-church type of Christians. He is the sort of Christian that doesn't mind who knows that he goes to church, believes in God, reads the Bible and prays (etc, etc). In fact, 'Damnation Dominic' is a Christian who believes in 'Witnessing' and it is this simple, even commendable desire to tell others about God and all things Christian that has earned him his nickname ('Damnation' isn't his real name – in case you thought he had very unloving parents!) and which has made him a Yard Health Hazard.

Each morning break-time 'Damnation Dominic'

can be seen – and heard – 'Witnessing' in the yard. His tactics are simple enough. He arrives on the scene about two minutes after the bell has rung for the start of break, clutching his large black Bible under his arm. He will pause briefly to survey the assembled masses and select a victim – usually a small, isolated Year Niner. 'Damnation' will approach his target and introduce himself with an opening line which usually goes something like, 'Hi. If you fell from the top of the ropes in the sports hall this afternoon would you go to heaven or hell?' You see, 'Damnation' likes to be loving and tactful when he first meets someone!

The small Year Niner usually looks a bit blank – possibly because she has never considered the possibility of either heaven OR hell lying at the foot of the ropes in the sports hall – and responds with a vague, 'Uh?'

Undaunted, 'Damnation' takes this response as encouragement to continue his 'Witnessing' and attempts to clarify the situation by asking, 'Are you covered by the blood of Jesus?'

Light dawns on the small Year Niner's face as she hastens to explain that the stain on the front of her school top is jam that has squirted out of her break-time doughnut, and not blood at all.

'Damnation' now makes his final contribution to the salvation of this small Year Niner's soul by explaining that 'streams of living water can be found in room 19 any Friday lunch-time for those who are thirsty enough to seek it.' The small Year Niner, who did not even realise that there were taps in room 19, never mind streams, is a little interested by this offer but explains that her

*'Damnation' likes to be loving and tactful
when he first meets someone!*

mum never lets her drink the water at school and always provides her with a carton of fruit juice which keeps her going through the day.

'Damnation' now feels good that this small Year Niner has been 'Witnessed' to and moves on to his next victim. Not much of a 'Peril' maybe, but if you see him moving in your direction I suggest that you start moving in the opposite one. (Or, you could pretend that you have just been beamed down from outer space and that you don't understand a word he's saying – which is at least partly true!)

The really important bit

The Bible does have quite a bit to say about Christians – all Christians – being witnesses for Jesus, BUT it doesn't have very much at all to say about the sort of 'Witnessing' being done by 'Damnation Dominic'. A good Bible passage to look at to understand real Christian witnessing is 1 Peter 3:14–16.

'... Do not be afraid of anyone, and do not worry. But have reverence for Christ in your hearts, and honour him as Lord. Be ready at all times to answer anyone who asks you to explain the hope you have in you, but do it with gentleness and respect. Keep your conscience clear, so that when you are insulted, those who speak evil of your good conduct as followers of Christ will be ashamed of what they say.'

These verses mention six important things about telling others about Jesus:

1   'Do not be afraid of anyone but have reverence for Christ.' This was about the only thing that 'Damnation Dominic' got right! He certainly wasn't afraid of what people thought of him! Sometimes, though, we can be so afraid of what other people think that we shut up rather than speak up. What do you really think is more important, disappointing your 'friends' by 'going all religious on them' or disappointing Jesus by failing to stand up for him? If your friends really care about their friendship with you, they won't mock your beliefs.

2   'Be ready ... to answer ...' Probably if 'Damnation Dominic' had bothered to talk to people and get to

know them a bit before preaching at them, he would have discovered that they would want to ask him some questions about what he believed. When you meet someone who cares deeply about something, you probably will want to ask them questions about why they care so much. If your true friends know that you're a Christian, sooner or later they'll want to know something about your faith. 'What's your church like?' 'Isn't the Bible hard to read?' 'How can Jesus be alive today if he died 2,000 years ago?' etc, etc. Real witnessing is more about answering friends' questions than telling strangers things that they aren't interested in.

3 'Be ready ... to explain ...' This is where so many Christians come off the rails. They quite simply cannot explain WHY they believe WHAT they believe, and so rather than admit their ignorance about their own faith, they just shut up. For instance you probably know that Christians believe that Jesus came alive again after being dead and buried for three days. But WHY do we believe that? Are there good reasons to believe it? Isn't there a better explanation for Jesus' body disappearing from the grave?

You also know that Christians base everything that they believe on what the Bible says. But again, WHY? Is every word in the Bible really straight from the mouth of God? Hasn't it been changed over the years to say different things from what the original writers intended? This is a REALLY IMPORTANT question, because if we cannot believe the Bible then we can just believe what we like (as most people who don't have much of a faith do) and reject what we don't like.

Hopefully you're beginning to see why it's important for you to be able to explain what you believe, and why you believe it. You'll probably need to do a bit of work for this! Spend a bit of time at your local Christian bookshop looking at books that help you find the answers to your questions. Keep pestering your parents (if they are Christians), or your church leader or youth leader for answers, and listen carefully to what they say.

A final word of warning on this point – don't be disappointed if the answer has to be, 'I don't know.' There are some things that God hasn't told us, and therefore we don't know. For example, we don't know exactly how God made the world, but that doesn't stop us believing that he DID make the world. Non-Christians (if they are honest) have to say that they don't know how the world and life was made; they've got loads of ideas (which they call 'theories') but they do not and cannot KNOW FOR SURE. All they can do is to look at the evidence and decide what they're going to believe. Looking at the evidence leads many scientists to believe that God made the world, whereas other scientists look at the same evidence and believe that it all happened by chance and that the world, the solar system, you and me are all just the result of a lucky string of enormous flukes!

4   '… do it with gentleness and respect.' Witnessing isn't about ramming your opinions and beliefs down someone else's ear trumpet, but gently explaining what you believe. Witnessing should never become an excuse for a heated argument; if things are moving

in that direction it's better to end the conversation sooner rather than later. You can always respect someone else's viewpoint without necessarily agreeing with it.

5 'Keep your conscience clear ...' There are no guarantees that people will believe what you believe about God, Jesus, the Bible etc. (That does not, of course, mean that they are right and you are wrong!)

However, one thing that's almost guaranteed is that if the things that you do don't match up to the things that you say, your friends will soon point that out to you!

If you talk about believing the Bible to be true and then go out and pick on someone who you don't get on with, your friends may remind you that the Bible has something to say about Christians loving their enemies! Witnessing is as much about showing people Christianity in the way we live as it is about explaining Christianity by the things that we say. (More on this in the next chapter.)

6 Be prepared to be insulted. You know and I know that not everyone will agree with you. This is usually because they've never thought much about Christianity and the only opinions that they have got are ones that they've picked up from their parent(s) or the TV. (Have you noticed how Christians on TV are usually the 'wet' ones?) So, when you start talking about Christianity or church or the Bible, probably the only answers that your friends have got are based on what they've heard from others, like 'It's all just made

up', or 'Jesus never really existed'.

If you then try to ask them WHY they believe that 'it's all made up' they won't have the foggiest idea and may get a bit abusive and say things like, 'Only sad people believe that load of junk.' All they're doing is trying to hide their own ignorance about Jesus and the Bible by being rude to you!

Being insulted occasionally is all part of the package deal with real witnessing – no witness, no insult.

Survival strategy!

1 Never imagine that one day it'll be really easy to witness. It DOES get easier, but the longer you keep your mouth shut about Jesus the harder it becomes to speak out.

2 Write down all the difficult questions that you don't feel you have an answer for and try to find a person or a book that helps you answer them.

3 Pray every day that God will fill you with the Holy Spirit so that you have more courage to speak up for Jesus.

4 Never feel a failure if you have to admit that you don't know the answer to a friend's question. It's better to admit that you don't know and then go away to find out the answer, then to make up an answer that isn't true!

5 Don't get drawn into pointless arguments. Try to

learn to tell the difference between people who are just wanting to have a row and people who REALLY want to know more about Jesus.

6   If you have a good Christian friend, you could always practise witnessing by one of you pretending to be an interested non-Christian and the other being themselves. The one who is 'playing' the role of the non-Christian should ask all the usual questions that your friends may ask, and the one who is being the Christian should attempt to answer. After a few questions and answers swap roles, and then discuss how convincing the Christian's answers were to the non-Christian.

7   Don't believe that you have to understand everything about Christianity before you can start explaining what you believe to your friends. Start with what you DO know – nobody understands everything!

Think about it

1   Write down the name of one friend who you think may be interested in knowing a bit more about what you believe as a Christian. Pray for an opportunity to speak to them (and then look out for the opportunity during the week).

2   Which do you care about more – keeping in with your friends or keeping in with Jesus?

Loving the Jesus way

(How to care like Jesus)

I don't think I've told you about Mr Grovey our drama teacher yet, have I? We all call him Mr Groovy – which he isn't, but it usually gets a laugh. (From the rest of the class, not from Mr Grovey.)

Mr Grovey is very thin. He has a bald head and a long beard, the combined effect of which is to make it appear as though his head is stuck on upside down. Like all teachers, he uses the phrase 'Right then' all the time. ('Right then, quieten down', 'Right then, let's see that group's work', 'Right then, who turned the lights off?' etc, etc.) He is actually a very good drama teacher, and because ALL drama lessons are practical, they make a welcome change from the routines of writing, reading and watching videos, which are the usual diet in most other subjects.

Mr Grovey likes to appear cool and trendy (as do most teachers under 30), but for Mr Grovey the attempt at an up-to-date image is ruined by his liking for wearing highly-patterned, sleeveless pullovers of the sort seen hanging in charity shops all over Britain.

Anyway, in order to get our interest at the start of each lesson he usually involves us in a silly game of some sort, and I still clearly remember the drama lesson when, thanks to David Smith (alias Dude D), the 'warm up' game went horribly wrong.

The instructions were clear enough. 'Right then, we'll start with a concentration exercise.' (Posh name for silly game!) 'Right then,' Mr Grovey bellowed, 'I'll call out an instruction like this: "Let's all hop on one leg," OK? Whenever an instruction starts with the words "Let's all" everyone *must* do it. But if I just say, "Hop on one leg," you should ignore the instruction. All clear? Right then, "Let's all touch all four walls of the drama studio."'

Immediately everyone charged around the room attempting to be the first to touch all the walls. 'Right then, sit down.' A few people sat on the floor (no chairs in the drama studio) and jumped straight to their feet again as an outbreak of jeering laughter told them that they'd got it wrong. And so the game, er... exercise, continued until Mr Grovey ran out of ideas AND made his big mistake at one and the same time.

'Right then, I've called out enough instructions, now I'll point to one of you and you must make up the instruction to be obeyed in just the same way as I have been doing. All right?' It was all right, so he pointed at Darren, who after a moment's thought said, 'Let's all take our shoes off' – which we did, amidst much good humoured nose-holding. So far so good, but Mr Grovey then pointed at David Smith (Dude D), who without the need for any thought whatsoever said, 'Let's all throw our shoes at Mr Grovey.' There was only the slightest of pauses for communal reflection before 29 pairs of shoes were duly launched at the teacher in charge.

To say that Mr Grovey was not amused is a bit of an understatement. I have rarely, if ever, seen a teacher

Twenty-nine pairs of shoes were launched at the teacher in charge.

whose flabber was so gasted. I won't bore you with the details of what happened next but the exercise was over and so was Dude D's participation in the lesson. He spent the rest of the double period seated at a desk in the corridor, copying chunks of Shakespeare's plays onto pieces of file paper.

After a suitably stern telling off from Mr Grovey (whose bald head always got redder the angrier he became) the lesson moved on to the next phase. 'Right then, get into pairs, please.' A simple enough request, you might think, but one that always caused complaint and argument.

The reason for the complaint was that given the even numbers in the class (now that Dude D was in the corridor!), someone had to work with Bryan

Smart. And no one wanted to. It wasn't Bryan's fault; he couldn't really help the fact that he didn't fit in, that he looked, well... strange, or that he was at the back of the queue when the brains were handed out. Nobody ever volunteered to work with Bryan, so Mr Grovey always had to force someone, usually by threatening something terrible if they refused.

As Mr Grovey searched the room for a suitable candidate to partner Bryan this week, unhappily his eye fell on me (not literally of course, it's just a way of saying 'he looked at me'!). My heart sank (again, not literally!) as I heard him say, 'Right then, I'm sure you'll work with Bryan today, won't you, David?'

The really important bit

If you had to fill in the gap at the end of the following sentence, what would you put? Have a go.

Being a Christian is all about learning to

_____

OK. How did you complete the sentence? No points if you wrote:
'eat spaghetti with chopsticks,'
or
'juggle soot blindfolded.'

Two points if you mentioned praying, reading the Bible, knowing God or anything along those lines, but for the purposes of this chapter you get a score of 5... yes, 5 points, if you mentioned respecting and caring for other people.

As mentioned in the chapter on 'Teachers!', the Bible has a lot of things to say about how we get on with other people. It keeps using this word, LOVE. In fact if one thing marks out a Christian as being different it should be this thing called 'love'. Not the sort of love that you see in films when the big hairy hero takes his girlfriend in his arms, half suffocates her with a big slobbering kiss and then says, 'I love you, Ermentrude.' No, when you read the word 'love' in the Bible it means something completely different; you don't have to hug anyone, kiss anyone or call them Ermentrude to love them the Jesus way.

The first thing to learn about Jesus' love is that it's available to everybody, 24 hours a day; it's not only for wealthy, good-looking boffins. In fact the people who Jesus chose to spend time with, to care for and even to heal weren't the 'successful' people, but the Bryan Smarts of his day. People like Zacchaeus for example.

OK, so Zacchaeus was clever, but that was about all he had going for him. He was short, and deeply unpopular with everyone because he had cheated them out of their money when he collected their taxes for the Romans. Even Mr Grovey would never have got anyone to work in a pair with Zacchaeus!

Now Jesus came to town one day and everyone – including Zacchaeus – wanted to get a look at this healer they'd heard so much about. Zacchaeus knew he wouldn't get a very good look at Jesus because he was too short to see over the heads of the crowd, so he shinned up a tree. All went according to plan and as Jesus came into view Zacchaeus could see him clearly.

Just as Jesus and the following crowd passed under

Zacchaeus' perch, Jesus stopped and looked straight up at him. Zacchaeus' heart must have missed a beat as all the crowd started telling Jesus who he was, and how he'd regularly cheated them out of their money. They told Jesus how he was getting richer and richer as they got poorer and poorer, and how he didn't have any pity even on people who really couldn't afford to pay.

Zacchaeus probably gritted his teeth and waited for a great long telling off from Jesus. He must have heard how Jesus was concerned for poor people and how he always welcomed the chance to correct people like Zacchaeus who were living wrongly. But... what was Jesus saying? Perhaps Zacchaeus could hardly hear because of the row the crowd was making: 'Hurry down, Zacchaeus, because I must stay in your house today.'

Oh, wow! Jesus having tea at the home of a cheating thief!! Whatever next? But this is the whole point about Jesus' love: it went out to everyone. Jesus said if someone is another Christian – love them. If someone is a friend – love them. If someone is an enemy – love them. If someone is a lonely cheat stuck up a tree – love them. If someone is a 'Bryan Smart' (and you've got them in your school) – love them. You don't have to LIKE the things that they do or say to LOVE them; Jesus certainly didn't like Zacchaeus' cheating, but he loved Zacchaeus! (You can read Zacchaeus' story for yourself in Luke 19:1–10.)

Just stop and think about this a minute. If Jesus had been in your class for drama, who would he have chosen to work with in a pair?

Loving the Jesus way is explained a lot more fully in the Bible, in 1 Corinthians 13:1–8.

'I may be able to speak the languages of men and even of angels, but if I have no love, my speech is no more than a noisy gong or a clanging bell. I may have the gift of inspired preaching; I may have all knowledge and understand all secrets; I may have all the faith needed to move mountains – but if I have no love, I am nothing. I may give away everything I have, and even give up my body to be burnt – but if I have no love, this does me no good.

'Love is patient and kind; it is not jealous or conceited or proud; love is not ill-mannered or selfish or irritable; love does not keep a record of wrongs; love is not happy with evil, but is happy with the truth. Love never gives up; and its faith, hope, and patience never fail.'

So let's just use this passage to make a 'Loving The Jesus Way At School' checklist. See how you get on.

1   I am patient with the Bryan Smarts of this world. Y/N
2   I am kind to the people at school who others laugh at. Y/N
3   I am not jealous of people who do things better than I can. Y/N
4   I don't have to boast about things that I do well. Y/N
5   I am not ill-mannered, even to unpopular teachers! Y/N
6   I am prepared to share my possessions with people who have less than I do. Y/N
7   I am willing to forgive people who have upset me and do not bear grudges against them. Y/N
8   I am not happy when something unfair happens to

someone else, and I try to stand up for what is right. Y/N

9 I never give up on people – even those who have let me down in the past. Y/N

Well, how did you get on? If you're like most of us, you've still got a fair way to go! But don't let your failures put you off trying harder. Just think how much of a better place school would be if EVERYONE loved the Jesus way! No more arguing. No more people left out and laughed at for being different. No more hurtful comments about people's looks. Of course it is extremely unlikely that EVERYONE will start loving the Jesus way, but that's no reason why YOU shouldn't start. Here to get you started is a ...

Survival strategy!

1 Think about your class and year group. Who are the people without many friends? Aim to be a better friend to just one of them, starting from today!

2 When your class moves from lesson to lesson, look for anyone walking on their own and walk with them.

3 When other people are taking the mickey out of someone else, try to imagine how they feel about it. Don't join in if it's getting hurtful.

4 Be prepared to stand up for what's right when something wrong is being done to, or said about someone.

5   Remember Jesus' Golden Rule: 'Do to others just what you want them to do for you.'

6   If your class is told to divide into groups by the teacher, keep a look-out for people who aren't in a group and invite them into yours.

7   Lunch-times can go on for ever if you have no friends and no one invites you to join in. Look out for anyone standing around on their own, and if possible try to involve them in what you're doing.

Think about it

1   Make a list of words that describe how you think Bryan Smart would feel about coming to school each day.

2   Write down a prayer for any 'Bryan Smarts' known to you.

Bethany Buckle fancies you

(Girlfriends, boyfriends and 'justgoodfriends')

The news came as a complete surprise. Bethany Buckle? Me? Surely there must be some mistake! Whatever could Bethany Buckle see in me? Perhaps the messenger had delivered the information to the wrong person. Maybe it was intended for Darren White or even Richard Morrison... but not me.

I certainly wanted it to be true because I was the only boy (well, nearly the only boy) in our class never to have had a girlfriend and I was beginning to feel a bit left out. But what should I do now that I'd been told about Bethany's feelings? There were several options that occurred to me:

1   Go to find her at lunch-time, throw my arms around her and promise my never-ending lifelong devotion.
2   Slip a notice into the Head's assembly announcements, asking her to marry me.
3   Quietly pass her a note in our next lesson asking if I could sit next to her on the bus, on the way home tonight.

I sat and pondered these options for some time before deciding that numbers 1 and 2 were probably a bit over the top (especially if it WAS Darren White that she really fancied!). Plan 3 it was then. Right, now what to put in the note?

How should I begin? 'Dear Bethany' er... 'Dearest Bethany' er... no, I know, Bethany's into poetry; it'd really impress her if I made my note into a poem! It took several attempts to get it right, but in the end I felt proud of my literary effort.

My fairest BB
From you to me
A message came today

Did I get it right
Or was it for D White?
'For me,' oh do please say.

I like your long hair
It touches the chair
Of you I would make a fuss

If you want to hold hands
Or flick elastic bands
Sit next to me on the school bus (tonight).

Poem by DL for BB

(In all honesty I didn't really think that she would want to flick elastic bands but I couldn't think of what else to rhyme with 'hands'.) Apart from that, I had said more or less what I wanted to say in a way that I thought Bethany could not fail to admire. The next problem was how to

Whatever could Bethany Buckle see in me?

deliver it, since I sat at the back in English (our next lesson) and Bethany sat at the front – which was how I knew that her hair touched her chair!

The lesson had started and I still didn't know how to deliver my masterpiece. I considered simply passing it forward, but some idiot would probably open it and read it out to the whole class, or else it would get intercepted by Mrs Burton who was the last person I wanted to read it. No, somehow I had to cut out the middlemen and middle-women. My final solution to the problem was a bit risky, but not as risky as the alternatives – or so I thought!

I was readily acknowledged as the Class Paper Aeroplane Making Champion (once constructing a complicated four-wing design which flew 12 metres in a dead straight line) and so I decided to put my skills to good use. Folding the sheet containing the poem into what I hoped was the perfect paper plane, I waited until Mrs Burton's back was turned and I launched the message-bearing missile in Bethany's direction. It flew dead straight, and was just about to begin its descent towards Bethany's desk when Jason Drew, who was sitting immediately behind Bethany, put his hand up to ask a question. The plane hit his raised arm which deflected its flight path, onto the desk of Rebecca Bradshaw.

Rebecca (or 'Becky' as everyone calls her) picked up the plane and, noticing that there was writing on it, slowly unfolded it. There was a slight delay as she read it then her head slowly turned in my direction and she gave me the biggest grin I'd ever seen. What was going on? Oh no... light slowly dawned. 'Becky Bradshaw'... 'BB'..!

My brain began to overheat at the sheer scale of the disaster that had just overtaken me. Becky thought that she was the 'BB' whose hand I wanted to hold on the bus tonight. Aaargh! To be fair, Becky was all right – in her way – but she was no Bethany. Bethany was fun, a laugh to be with, oh, and, er, gorgeous. Becky was, well, sort of ordinary if you know what I mean. Oh grief, pain and stress – what was I going to do?

The really important bit

The Bible doesn't have a great deal to say about boys and girls going out with girls and boys. People officially became adults at the age of 12 in Bible times, and at that age, or shortly after, their parents arranged who they would marry! The Jewish law expected a boy to get married between the age of 13 and 18 to a Jewish girl aged 12-and-a-half to 15! You can see that there's no point in the Bible writers wasting ink explaining how to go out with someone who fancies you when 'going out' and 'fancying' weren't part of the way that they did things then!

HOWEVER, the Bible does have a load of things to say about how to treat other people and about how to build friendships. A lot of this good advice is easy to apply to girl/boy relationships. Here are a few 'Bible Bits' to help you understand friendships a bit better:

1   'Good looks or cool clothes can be misleading. What's really important is whether or not someone loves God' (my version of Proverbs 31:30).

    If you do decide to go out with a non-Christian, sooner or later (and it'll probably be sooner) your different beliefs will come between you. So think carefully!

2   'Beauty is only skin-deep. What's really important is the sort of person you are' (my version of 1 Peter 3:4).

    TV programmes, adverts and magazines always show a certain sort of person as attractive. There's a certain shape that's shown as the 'right way' to look

– usually slim for girls and tall and broad-shouldered for guys! There are certain sorts of clothes that make you an 'OK person' (like combats or Nike trainers).

There's an old saying that goes 'you should never judge a book by its cover', and it's true: you should never judge a person by their looks. Deciding that you want to go out with someone because they happen to fit into this year's idea of what's gorgeous is stupid. The Bible's right (surprise, surprise), you should always try to get to know what a person is *really* like before deciding whether or not you want to build a deep friendship with them.

3 You must not be envious of your friends. This is something that we can read about in the Ten Commandments (see Exodus 20:17).

It's always a great temptation to look around, see what other people are doing or what they've got and want to be like them. Maybe you're the only boy/girl in the class who has never been out with anyone – or at least, it seems that way to you! But whether or not that's true doesn't matter.What does matter is that you're YOU. What your friends do is up to them and you shouldn't feel that you have to copy them. It's not wrong or odd to be different, in fact it's far wiser to think things out for yourself than to just blindly and unthinkingly follow the crowd.

If everyone else has got boy or girlfriends, so what? No one says that YOU have to, and if your main reason for wanting a close friendship is to be like everyone else then it won't be much of a friendship anyway!

4   'Respect everyone ...' (1 Peter 2:17).

One of the words that the Bible uses most often to describe a Christian's relationships is this word 'respect'. What does it mean to 'respect' someone? The Concise Oxford Dictionary (which, without a doubt, you read every night before going to sleep...!) says that if you respect someone you will avoid:

– degrading them (putting them down)
– insulting them
– injuring them
– offending them
– tempting them
– corrupting them.

It also says that if you respect someone you will 'treat them with consideration' and 'esteem them' (think of them as valuable).

All relationships should be built on respect but, perhaps in particular, close friendships should be especially respectful! Just wanting to go out with someone because they 'fancy you' or because you 'fancy them' just isn't enough. Do you really care for them? Do you really respect them?

---

5   'Don't be selfish; don't live to make a good impression on others ...' (Philippians 2:3 in the Living Bible).

What's your *real* reason for wanting to go out with that person? It's always wrong to want a special friendship with someone just so that you feel better about yourself or so that others are impressed.

---

6   'Don't just think about your own affairs, but be interested in others too ...' (Philippians 2:4 in the Living Bible).

Even when you do start going out with someone special, don't spend ALL your time with them. Keep good friendships with everyone. If you and your girl/boyfriend are at youth group – talk to other people and take part in the activities. It makes things awkward for everyone if you both act like someone has super-glued you together!

Survival strategy!

1 Don't feel a failure if you've never had a boyfriend or girlfriend. It doesn't mean that you never will and it doesn't make you odd. Be patient, your time will come!

2 Be a good friend to as many people as possible – boys and girls.

3 Never judge someone by the way they look.

4 Sometimes close friendships can go wrong or get a bit hurtful. Try to find an adult (parent, youth leader, etc) who you trust enough to be able to talk to about all of your friendships. It's important that you're prepared to listen to their advice too!

5 Never look at other people as 'things' to own for a while and then dump when you're fed up with them. People of whatever shape and size are all created and loved by God and all deserve respect (see above).

6 Don't be conned by your school friends or by what

you see on TV! The most important part of boy/girl relationships is NOT holding hands, cuddling and kissing! In fact as I've said above, that's really the least important part. Friendship is about caring for the other person, respecting the other person, sharing your interests with the other person, enjoying just being with the other person – but not about suffocating the other person with big slobbering kisses!

Think about it

1 What do you think the difficulties could be if a Christian went out with a non-Christian?

2 Make a list of words or phrases that describe things you think are important in building good relationships with people, eg enjoying being together, trust. Then put them into practise!

Just a game?

(What about the occult?)

I don't know whether you realise this or not, but your school has a prospectus. A prospectus is a sort of handbook which is supposed to tell you and your parents everything that you need to know about surviving at your school. I say 'supposed to tell you', because there are always important bits of information missed out of the school prospectus; for example, they never tell you that:

'No loo door in this school has a lock!'
or,
'A recording of the school's brass band is used in place of warning sirens on all local police vehicles.'

No, nothing so useful or interesting is ever included. Instead, the average school prospectus is usually full of statements like this:

'Every pupil at Kidminster Green is cared for by a personal tutor who remains with the tutor group throughout the pupil's school career. At the start of each school day there is a 20-minute tutorial time, during which personal, social and moral values are discussed within the tutor group.'

You know, I think whoever wrote the prospectus of Kidminster Green should be taken to court and charged

The variety of activities that my class regard as 'useful'.

with 'Gross Deceit of Parents and Pupils' because what actually takes place in the first 20 minutes of the school day bears absolutely *no* relation to what the prospectus says should happen. Take my tutor group as a totally typical example of the point that I'm trying to make.

The bell rings at 8.45 and we all gather at the door of our tutor base. Actually it would be more accurate to call it a tutor 'hut' since our class is based in one of those 'temporary' classrooms that sprouted up around schools all over the country about twenty years ago. Ours hasn't been decorated since it was erected because every year is supposed to be its 'last' year. A few half-hearted attempts at brightening the place up with posters have been made by a succession of teachers, but it doesn't really help because the huts suffer from terminal damp and the posters quickly go all brown and blotchy, making the general appearance of the hut's interior more, not less, gloomy.

We usually have to queue up in the rain because Mr Barnes – our 'Supa-Tuta' – keeps the door locked until his arrival, to prevent vandalism (although there are those who think that a spot of creative vandalism would smarten the place up a bit!). He arrives without the key and sends a runner to the office to retrieve it, while he calls the register in the rain.

The runner soon returns and we all shuffle soggily into the hut. Mr Barnes usually then says something like, 'Right then, get on with something useful. I've got a lot of preparation to do before first period.' At this point it's really interesting to note the variety of activities that the members of my class regard as 'useful'. Here are a sample few:

1 Copying last night's homework from the class 'mega-brain'.
2 Staring out of the window.
3 Cleaning dirty fingernails with straightened out paper clips.
4 Writing 'DF 4 SM' on the back of your hand.
5 Hiding Bryan Smart's bag in the stock cupboard.
6 Eating your packed lunch.
7 Hiding Bryan Smart's coat in the stock cupboard.
8 Seeing how red you can go by holding your breath.
9 Hiding Bryan Smart in the stock cupboard.
10 Picking your nose.

Now I suppose some of these ARE useful (although I'm not sure which ones) but I am sure that none of them help develop my 'personal, moral and social values' as claimed by the school prospectus.

To be fair there was a week when Mr Barnes spotted this and suggested that, seeing as how we all wasted our tutor time (WE wasted it – I like that!), we should bring in a board game next week and he'd organise a sort of tournament.

Well, several people did bring in board games, but Mr Barnes was 'too busy' to organise us, so we just joined in with whatever we fancied. Some played Monopoly (which is a daft game to try to play in 20 minutes – even my mum couldn't go bankrupt in that time) and others joined several games together and invented a new one which they called 'Scruvial Cluedopolybats'.

There was one small group though who went through to the store area at the back of the hut and got on with something really quietly. I thought that they were swapping last night's French homework but it turns out that they were playing a game called 'Ouija'. Apparently they all had to sit in a circle and put their hands on the playing board. They then asked the board questions and a pointer on the board moved to either 'yes' or 'no' to give them an answer. The girls who were using it reckoned that they were contacting 'the spirit world' but I thought it was all a big con trick. Anyway, whatever, it got pretty popular for a bit before everyone got bored with it and went back to staring out of the window and hiding Bryan Smart (and his accessories) in the stock cupboard.

So that's tutor time at Kidminster Green; so much for the school prospectus, eh?

The really important bit

'Games' like 'Ouija' are not really games at all. They

really do try to contact the invisible 'spirit world' that surrounds us all.

Many people today only believe in what they can see and touch and so they don't believe in spirits, demons, angels or even God! (Despite what they may say, everyone DOES believe in invisible things – no one doubts the existence of wind, electricity, love or toothache, even though no one has ever seen any of those things!)

Anyway, the important thing isn't whether people believe in something or not – the important thing is whether it's actually true or not. We might really believe that smoking cigarettes does us no harm. We might ignore all the warnings and even try to convince other people that lung cancer doesn't really exist. The point is that whether we believe it or not, and whether we convince our friends that we're right or not, doesn't alter the fact that smoking cigarettes may cause lung cancer.

In just the same way a lot of your friends may choose not to believe in God... or Jesus... or angels... or evil spirits, and they may even try to convince you that they are right! But are they?

As far as the Bible is concerned there is very definitely a real but invisible 'spirit world' which surrounds us all. The Bible is quite clear that God is a spirit and that he commands an action force of good spirits (usually called angels). And this 'spirit world' has its baddies. God has an invisible enemy, Satan, who, although very evil, is greatly inferior to God. Satan also commands a spirit action force: an evil one of 'demons' and 'evil spirits'.

The Bible is quite clear that these evil spirits (and

the things that they do) are dangerous. It warns us that we should not have anything to do with them or with people who try to use their powers.

Activities like 'Ouija' really are trying to contact spiritual powers – but the power comes from evil spirits, not God's spirits (or dead people). Evil spiritual powers; let's look at that name more closely:

EVIL – because they are only interested in damaging our lives, not in helping us.

SPIRITUAL – because they are not people; they are real invisible beings, or spirits.

POWERS – because IF WE LET THEM they really DO have the power to hurt us and damage our lives.

So how can these evil spiritual powers affect our lives? These powers are very crafty and will look for any opportunity to get at us. If we get involved in activities which claim to contact hidden powers (another word for 'hidden' is 'occult') – then, often without meaning to, we open our minds to those harmful influences.

Remember that anything that claims to work by means of spiritual powers needs to be looked at carefully. There are only two sources of spiritual power: God and Satan. Every invisible spirit is either on God's side or on Satan's side.

Lots of activities that need a spiritual power to make them work are actually outlawed by God in the Bible, so any spiritual power being used in them is clearly not from him but is from Satan; God wouldn't ban something that he'd created for our good!

The Bible warns us against getting involved with occult activities. Some of those activities might include: ouija boards, astrology (horoscopes), mind reading, levitation, palm reading, tarot cards, seances.

You may not have heard of some of these things, but one day you probably will. Just remember that the invisible spiritual force that makes them work is evil and harmful, so leave them all well alone.

We may not understand the occult (hidden) powers that lie behind these activities but be warned – they are REAL and they are HARMFUL.

Take, for example, the true story of John:

John was invited by some friends to 'play' with a ouija board. He'd never done it before but thought it sounded like harmless fun.

During the 'game', the board predicted the death of the best friend of someone taking part.

John thought no more about it – until, two weeks later, HIS best friend was killed in a freak motorbike accident.

During the months that followed, John's life was miserable. He blamed himself for the death of his friend, thinking that if he hadn't used the ouija board, perhaps his friend would still be alive.

At times John felt like taking his own life as a kind of token repayment for the life of his friend.

Satan was probably delighted to cause John so much guilt and misery. Satan is interested in bringing misery... suffering... pain... and guilt into our lives. Think about it! You don't want to run the risk of someone like that getting at you, so steer right away from any of the sorts of activities listed above.

Survival strategy!

1 If you've never been involved in any of the activities listed above then DON'T... DON'T... DON'T!! Even if your friends urge you to join in... DON'T... DON'T... DON'T!!

2 Don't be frightened of evil spirits. They cannot just choose to hurt you, you have to give them the chance (for example by joining in activities like those listed above) – so don't!

3 If you have been involved in any occult activities in the past then DON'T PANIC, just read on.

4 Although Satan has the power to hurt people who get too close to him, his power is not unstoppable! Jesus Christ has the power to destroy all the harmful effects of what Satan tries to do. This is what the Bible has to say on the subject:
'The Son of God [Jesus] appeared for this very reason, to destroy what the Devil [Satan] had done' (1 John 3:8).
'If the Son [Jesus] sets you free, then you will be really free' (John 8:36).

5 If you want a clean start, Jesus can give it to you! He can replace the negative influence of Satan with the positive power of God's Holy Spirit. So...

6 Pray to Jesus. Tell him how sorry you are for letting Satan influence your life. Ask him to 'throw out' anything harmful which may be affecting you.

7 Ask Jesus to fill your mind and spirit with his Holy Spirit.

8 Talk to an older Christian about your experiences. Show them this chapter of the book and ask them to pray with you. Ask for their advice about how to stay close to Jesus. This may seem like a hard thing to do, but if you've been involved with occult powers you really do need the help of an older Christian, so pluck up all your courage and... GO FOR IT!

Think about it

1 What will be your response if you get invited to play 'Ouija', have your palm read or use tarot cards?

2 Do you know anyone who is involved in these sorts of things? Pray that God would protect them from the evil spiritual powers that they are contacting.

Failed again!

(Overcoming failure)

Today was the day! This morning I had prayed for a chance to let my classmates know that I was a Christian, and I entered school determined to take the mask off my secret faith. I had been in the school for a term and a half now, and I had managed to duck and dive whenever questions about God came up (which, fortunately, was not very often anyway). Over the months since last September, there had been loads of Sundays when I had got all stirred up at church about telling my school friends that I was a Christian, but somehow it had just never happened. But today was the day! This Monday, Jesus was going to help me and I would be a witness, not a wimp.

Lining up to go into our tutor base with my friends, I was waiting for any opportunity. (Now that I was actually standing shoulder to shoulder with them, owning up to being a Christian didn't seem quite so easy as it had last night in church. Still, I had prayed for help and 'today was the day'.) I joined a crowd gathered around Nick Neutron, the class superbrain, who was sounding off about some scientific programme that he had seen on TV last night.

'It was totally cool, wasn't it?' he asked.

'What was?' I queried.

Nick took a deep breath and launched into his explanation. 'The way that presenter-bloke demonstrated

Nick took a deep breath and launched into his explanation.

that Newton's mechanistic view of the universe was not undermined by Einstein as commonly thought, but that the initial challenge to Newtonian physics began half a century before Einstein, with the discovery and development of the laws of thermodynamics. Of course, the second law...'

I interrupted. 'Nick, what on earth are you on about?' No sooner had I asked than I regretted the question passing my lips.

Nick continued, 'Well it all started with this German guy called Clausius who worked out that heat cannot pass from a cold body to a hot body – not without help anyway.'

Nick looked at me to see if this further clarification of his 'totally cool' programme had helped me. But the puzzled look on my face apparently didn't encourage him.

'Hang on!' I urged. 'You're telling me that someone became famous by working out that a cold body cannot pass heat to a hot body?'

This was an insult to my intelligence, and I felt it was my duty to point out the obvious flaws in the thermodynamic laws.

'First, Nick, if a body was a cold body it would, in all probability, be a dead body and so would be in no fit condition to pass anything to anyone.

'Second, strudelbrain, even if it was an alive cold body, by definition it would have no heat to pass to a hot body. Because if it had heat to go throwing about the place, it couldn't have been a cold body to start with.'

I was warming to my task (so to speak!) and continued, 'Thirdly, splurge-head, a hot body is probably a sick body – fever or something, I wouldn't wonder. So no sensible cold body would go anywhere near it in case it caught something.'

I looked at Nick triumphantly, expecting him to congratulate me on disproving the thermodynamic laws before school had even started. He didn't speak for a while. He just kind of looked at me. After a long pause, he spoke. 'You stupid, dim-witted, ignorant brickhead! I have never heard such a load of garbage. You've got no idea what you're talking about, yet you go burbling on as though you're some kind of scientific mastermind.'

To be honest, I was a bit disappointed with this response. But I comforted myself with the thought that it is quite common for a genius not to be recognised by his own friends. Anyway, at this point Mr Barnes, our tutor, arrived and ushered us into our places for registration. Once everyone was accounted for, a few notices were given out (band practise cancelled on Wednesday, humanities field trip money to be in by Friday, wheel trims from the Head's car to be returned immediately or else) and we were left to talk amongst ourselves until the bell went for assembly.

Nick was unwilling to let our previous conversation lie down and die, and the fact that ten minutes had passed since we'd finished talking had clearly not improved my intellectual standing in his eyes. In a voice heavy with sarcasm, he enquired, 'So, Scientist of the Year, if you weren't tuned into *Physics-Watch* last night – and you clearly were not – what were you watching on TV? *The Tweenies? Bob the Builder?*'

'Oh yeah, yeah. Very funny. If you must know, actually I...'

Actually I was in church but I couldn't admit that. Not now. Not to smart-alec Nick Neutron. He'd only have some sort of creepily smug response and make a huge joke about it at my expense. So I continued, 'Actually I didn't watch any TV last night. I... I went round to a mate's house and played computer games until about 9.30 and then went home, finished my homework and went to bed.'

Before Nick could answer, three long rings of the bell announced an impending assembly. As I trudged off to hear Dr Fiennes tell us about the character-building features of his recent research trip to Antarctica, I felt as miserable as when I'd accidentally dropped the chocolate flake from my 99 ice cream down the drain last summer.

There it was. My great opportunity to tell someone that I had been in church last night and I had blown it. And, to make it worse, I had told a lie. Two lies in fact, since I hadn't been at a friend's house and I hadn't done any homework. All my good intentions had come to nothing and first lesson hadn't even started yet. How could I be so feeble? How could I look God in the eye? I can't keep on going back to him and saying, 'Sorry, I messed up. But next time I'll do better', can I? He's heard that so many times I doubt that he even listens any more, much less believes that I really AM sorry and that I really DO mean to do better next time.

Oh gloom, stress and deep, deep guilt. Sure, 'today was the day'. Today was the day when I blew it – again.

The really important bit

One of the great things about the Bible is that God made sure it was filled with real-life stories. There are stories about kings, shepherds, fishermen, widows, teenagers, musicians, and doctors – and that's only a small fraction of the characters who get a mention in the Bible!

These real-life people did loads of different things. Many of them did big, impressive things. They built cities, conquered armies, fought lions with their bare hands, wrote books, healed the sick... The list could go on and on. But there is one thing that all of these great people had in common. There were times in their lives when they let God down, sometimes quite spectacularly.

Noah got drunk, Abraham got his wife's servant

pregnant, Jacob lied to his father, Moses committed murder. Person after person made mistakes and failed to live up to what God expected of them. But the really cool thing about God is that, although he never approved of the wrong things that these Bible characters did – and sometimes he let them suffer a bit as a result of their own mistakes – he was always ready to forgive someone who really regretted what they had done and who wanted to start again.

Forgiving isn't hard for God because that is how he is. He would find it far harder to bear a grudge or to keep a list of someone's sins on his personal organiser than he would to forget them. Get a load of this:

> 'The LORD is merciful and loving,
>> slow to become angry and full of constant love.
> He does not keep on rebuking;
>> he is not angry for ever.
> He does not punish us as we deserve
>> or repay us for our sins and wrongs.
> As high as the sky is above the earth,
>> so great is his love for those who honour him.
> As far as the east is from the west,
>> so far does he remove our sins from us.
> As a [good] father is kind to his children,
>> so the LORD is kind to those who honour him.
> He knows what we are made of;
>> he remembers that we are dust.'
> (Psalm 103:8–14)

Notice four things about God:

1   He is FULL of constant love!

Sure, some things make God angry. But his basic character is described by this word 'love'. He is not an angry God who is sometimes kind, but an amazingly kind God who sometimes (quite reasonably) gets angry!

The New Testament tells us that love 'does not keep a record of wrongs' – and neither does God! WE have a problem because we remember ALL our mistakes. So when we blow it yet again, it seems to us like yet another addition to a huge long line of failures. But when we have confessed a sin – told God that we really regretted our failure and asked him for help to be stronger next time – he forgets it. So, if we make the same mistake again, to God it's like the first time we've ever made it because he has already deleted the previous times from his memory bank!

All our guilt about the last time we blew it (and the time before) is a waste of worry because God forgot all about the last time (and the time before) when we said 'Sorry'.

2 He does NOT punish us as we deserve (ever!).

We might expect that a loving God would give us more than one chance to get things right, but just how patient is he prepared to be? How many times does he accept 'Sorry' for the same mistake?

It's all very well knowing that God will accept 'Sorry, I'll try harder' the first few times that we make a mistake. But, after several identical sins, surely God has every right to give up on us and look for someone who is a bit more reliable?

Peter had this problem about constantly forgiving the same person for the same thing, but from a different angle. He wanted to know how many times HE should forgive someone who had upset HIM. So he asked Jesus, 'Lord, if my brother keeps on sinning against me, how many times do I have to forgive him?

Seven times?' Peter probably thought that he was being pretty generous offering to forgive someone seven times for the same mistake. So imagine his shock when Jesus answered, 'Not seven times but seventy times seven'! (See Matthew 18:21–22) You can imagine Peter saying, 'But Jesus, I'll lose count!' and Jesus replying, 'Then you'll just have to keep on forgiving, in case!'

Jesus went on to explain to Peter that our forgiveness of people who do us wrong should be at least as generous as God's forgiveness of us when we let him down. This story tells us that if WE are told to forgive 'seventy times seven', then GOD must forgive at least seven hundred times seventy and probably nearer seven million times seventy thousand!

No matter how many times you have to say sorry for your failures, God would sooner forgive you than punish you!

3 He is kind to those who HONOUR HIM.

What does this mean? Well, it's all a matter of attitude. God sees a world of difference between someone who keeps making mistakes and couldn't really care less, and someone who keeps making mistakes and feels stressed out because they know they have let God down. If you honour God, you'll want to do what he likes, so you'll be disappointed when you let him down. It doesn't mean that a person who honours God will always get everything right (look at the list of God-honouring Bible failures above!) but it does mean that such a person will always WANT to do what God wants and will want to apologise sincerely when they let him down.

If you really do want to please God, God will be kind and forgive you – even if you do keep blowing it!

4   He knows what we are made of!

This is great news for all Christians – God knows how hard it is to be a human and how easy it is to get it all wrong. But how CAN God understand us humans? Easy!

First, he made us! He put us together and knows how we tick. So he knows how we feel, what upsets us and what sorts of things are likely to make us do things that we later regret. It's because he knows how we work, that he knows where our weaknesses are, and is able to be extra patient.

Second, God knows what it's like to be human because Jesus was God-AND-human. In the life of Jesus, God experienced the hassles of being human from the inside out. He knows what it feels like to be hurt, laughed at, rejected and tempted. Jesus himself never actually went so far as to sin, but his experiences on earth have made him incredibly understanding of the sorts of things that lead us to let him down. The Bible puts it this way:

'[Jesus] is able to understand our weaknesses. When he lived on earth, he was tempted in every way that we are, but he did not sin. Let us, then, feel free to come before God's throne. Here there is grace. And we can receive mercy and grace to help us when we need it' (Hebrews 4:15–16, International Children's Bible).

These four facts about God should be a GREAT encouragement to everyone who feels guilty about making the same mistake over and over again. God can handle it. (What he can't handle is people who make the same mistakes over and over again and who don't care about it!)

Different people struggle with different areas where they feel a constant failure. For some it may be letting God down by their failure to speak out for him. Others may feel bad because they can't stop swearing, or lying, or gossiping about other classmates. All these things ARE wrong, but God's heart of forgiving love is big enough to forgive you every single time you say sorry.

This is brilliant! But what about the next step? God can forgive any number of failures and mistakes, but how can you change so that the failures become less frequent? To help you, here's a...

Survival strategy!

1   Write a 'Reallywannabedifferent' statement.

Try and identify very specifically which recurring failure you want to overcome and in what way you want to change. Write this down on a piece of paper and put it where you'll see it first thing every day (eg in your Bible, with your Bible notes if you use them, or pinned on the wall by your bed).

For example, you might write:

'I reallywannabedifferent! I really want to stop being afraid of what other people think, and talk to someone at school about why I'm a Christian.'

'I reallywannabedifferent! I really want to get out of the habit of swearing at school.'

'I reallywannabedifferent! I really want to stop

chickening out and invite Steve to youth group.'

2 Copy out the Bible passage from Psalm 103 (on page 94) on another piece of paper and put it next to your 'Reallywannabedifferent' statement.

3 Each morning make sure that you pray for God's help in reaching your 'Reallywannabedifferent' goal that day.

4 Think carefully about the reasons for your frequent failures. Are there particular people who lead you into trouble? If so, try to spend less time with them. Are there particular times of the day when you feel you fail (like when you're just hanging around with your mates at lunch-time)? If so, take extra care and say an extra prayer at those times. Be on the alert and try even harder in the places where you fail most often.

5 Talk to someone else about your 'Reallywannabedifferent' statement. Go to an older Christian who you get on with and let them in on your struggles. Ask them to pray for you, and ask if they've got any bright ideas to help you. Give them permission to check up on you! Say 'I want you to ask me about once a week how I'm getting on.' The thought that someone else has permission to check up on you can be a great help in changing your behaviour!

6 At the end of each day read your 'Reallywannabedifferent' statement and be honest with yourself about how well you've done (or not!). Then read the bit

from Psalm 103 and tell God how you feel about your progress (or lack of it). Remember the four facts about God's forgiveness in this chapter and go to sleep with a clear conscience knowing that, if you have confessed your sin, God has been faithful and forgiven you – even if it's the 7,000,000,370,000th time!

Think about it

1   Think about your 'Reallywannabedifferent' statement and write it out here.

2   Do you know anyone else who is struggling to believe that God can forgive their constant failures? Pray for them and think how you could encourage them with some of the ideas from this chapter.

Remember – you're not alone

(Touching base with other Christians)

Twice a week we have an assembly and, as a rule, assemblies are about the only occasions that Christianity gets a mention at school. (I suppose RE lessons would be the only exception to this rule, but when you've got an RE teacher who doesn't believe in the existence of God and thinks that Jesus was an astronaut, there's a limit to how 'Christian' Religious Education really can be!)

Anyway, Friday's assembly is a 'whole school' event held in the school sports hall. As soon as the bell goes for the start of school we go to our tutor group rooms to drop off our bags and coats and then make straight for the hall. Arriving at the sports hall door we all (all being the 984 pupils in the school) remove our shoes and walk to the half square metre of floor allocated for each pupil, taking our shoes with us.

It took the combined brain power of the teachers quite a few weeks to arrive at this simple routine for getting into Friday assembly. The very first week we ever tried it (just after the sports hall had been built), the instruction was to go straight to the sports hall when the bell rang for the start of school. Understandably, perhaps, the novelty of a new event in the school's weekly calendar caused quite a stir, and about half of the school (the

There was the distinct possibility of serious injury being inflicted on the departing pupils.

younger, more excitable half) arrived at the sports hall early, before the supervising teachers had arrived from their early morning staff briefing. They charged straight into the hall, leaving muddy trails from their shoes all across the new sports hall floor and, using their bags as improvised seating, proceeded to sit down still wrapped in their coats.

At this point Mr Wilson, the Strict Deputy Head, arrived (every school with more than one Deputy Head has a 'Strict' one for telling you off and keeping order in assemblies, and a 'Friendly' one for helping you when you've been bullied). He surveyed the scene of human chaos and the mud patch that used to be the floor, raised his voice above the high-pitched din and yelled 'Who told you to come in here, you silly children? Get out immediately and take your bags with you.' He was, I think, not happy.

In fact, such was the sheer awesomeness of Mr Wilson's fury that, as one person, the whole assembled mass headed for the door at top speed. Unfortunately, just as they began to beat their hasty retreat, the bell for the start of school rang. This signalled the arrival of the half of the school that had NOT been early for assembly, who tried to enter the sports hall at the same time as the half that had just been thrown out tried to exit. Since the new arrivals were (mostly) larger than those trying to leave, the contest was not an even one and quite soon there was the chance of serious injury being inflicted on the departing Year 7 and 8 pupils.

Mr Wilson soon had the situation under control. He managed to get the whole school lining up in the four corridor approaches to the sports hall. New instructions were issued. Coats, bags and shoes were to be left in the corridors and not brought in to the hall.

There was a sense of urgency about proceedings now (the 15 minute assembly time was more than half over already) so everyone duly dropped bags, coats and shoes where they were, filed into the sports hall and sat on the floor for the assembly.

Mr Wilson, who was still almost beside himself with rage, spoke first. He spoke with the sort of quietly threatening tone that you ignored at your peril. He told us terrible tales of people being crushed in crowds, of school finances being wasted on unnecessary floor cleaning bills and of 'softies' who needed seats when there was a perfectly good floor to sit on (all the teachers were sitting on chairs around the edge of the sports hall at this point, but I don't think they took it personally). We all felt suitably got at.

The Head, who had obviously prepared a lengthy moralising talk for this historic first assembly in the new sports hall rose to his feet just as the bell for the end of assembly rang. He glanced nervously at his watch and made a hasty decision. 'Because of your ridiculous behaviour this morning I shall save most of what I wanted to say until next week, when I hope that we can have a more ordered start to the school assembly. However I would like to leave you with something to think about during the day. It's from the Bible, actually, and it would have formed a small part of what I wanted to say to you this morning; "Don't make friends with people who have hot, violent tempers. You might learn their habits and not be able to change."' Everyone's eyes shifted to Mr Wilson and wondered...!

We were hastily dismissed and only then did the staff realise the problems caused by 984 pupils searching for shoes, bags and coats in school corridors that looked like the after-effects of an explosion in an Oxfam shop. It was 9.45 before the last person was reunited with their property and it was rumoured that Mr Wilson took the rest of the day off to recover!

So there it was; our week's religious input. To be honest it didn't do much to encourage me to live for Jesus and I don't think it did anything at all for my non-Christian friends.

The really important bit

Is that the way that God intends it? The entire school's

Christian input restricted to two Bible verses on a Friday morning and the opinions of an RE teacher who doesn't even believe in God? No, it's not!

A Bible passage that you might imagine could have been set in a school yard (or assembly hall) is found in Matthew 9:36–38. Jesus has been travelling around and has got quite a reputation from his preaching and healing exploits. So many people wanted to get close to him that wherever he went he was followed by a crowd of people.

Perhaps anyone else would have got fed up with all the attention and been tempted to tell the crowds to go home and leave them alone. But not Jesus.

'As [Jesus] saw the crowds, his heart was filled with pity for them, because they were worried and helpless, like sheep without a shepherd.' He was really concerned for the crowds because he knew that he was their only hope. If he fumed and walked away from them, they had no one else to go to for help, advice and healing. I think that if Jesus stood in your school and looked around at the crowds he would feel exactly the same.

He would see loads of young people who are trying to learn how to make sense of life, trying to sort out what's right and what's wrong, trying to understand who they are and how to get on with people around them. The trouble is they're trying to understand life – life that was invented by God – without knowing much or anything at all about the inventor. It's a bit like trying to put together a Lego Technic kit without the instruction leaflet or cook a complicated meal without a recipe book; let's face it, it can't be done! In just the same way, a school full of people who have no real idea about life's inventor and designer are not likely to make a very wonderful job of sorting out what life IS all about –and they are certainly NOT going to be helped by two unexplained Bible verses in a weekly assembly!

So what can be done? Well, in the passage from Matthew's book about the life and times of Jesus, he tells us that after Jesus had been moved to pity because the crowd seemed so lost, he turned to his best friends and said:

'The harvest is large, but there are few workers to gather it in. Pray to the owner of the harvest [God] that he will send out workers to gather in his harvest.'

God's plan is for ordinary Christian people (the workers) to help the harvest (people who don't know God) to know who God is. Putting it more simply, it's all down to you and me! God's plan for introducing himself to people in your school involves YOU and all the other Christians in your school in starring roles.

God wants you to be so full of Jesus that you actually start acting like him. The things that you do become the things that he would do. The things that you say would be the things that he would say. The people that you hang around with would be the people that he would hang around with... and so on. If all the Christians in your school started acting like Jesus, then people wouldn't be dependent upon an occasional Christian assembly to teach them about God. In every class in every school there would be walking, talking visual aids showing what God thinks, does and says.

Let's be absolutely honest though and say that it's

not always going to be easy to try to live for Jesus at school. You see, in a school where most people aren't living for Jesus, it will soon become obvious that you're different, and not everybody will agree with what you believe. Some will say so: others may just ignore you. What *does* make living for Jesus at school a lot easier is to know that you're not alone; that there are other Christians who agree with what you believe and who can encourage you when the going gets a bit tough. It makes a lot of sense to meet with these other Christians so that you can all know and encourage one another. Perhaps the best way to do this regularly is to form a Christian group of some sort which meets in your school, maybe at lunch-time.

If your school already has a Christian group, get involved with it. If it hasn't, you might want to think about starting one. Here's some help to get you going...

Survival strategy!

1   Go online to www.schoolslive.org which is a website full of resources for Christian groups in schools. Find the 'New to schoolswork?' section where you can download a guide to starting a group. This will help you think through some important questions, such as:

'What is a school Christian group for?'
and
'What sort of group do we need at our school?'

2   Make a list of all the Christians you know of at your

school. Include pupils, teachers – even caretakers and dinner ladies.

3   Try to talk to some of the people on your list to explain that you're thinking of starting a Christian group in school. Explain what's in your mind and ask whether they'd be interested in helping start it or being a part of it when it gets going.

4   Talk to your church leader or youth leader and ask them for advice and prayer support.

5   Now the biggie! You will need to see the Head to ask for permission to meet in school and for a room to meet in. If you have a sympathetic teacher then their help will be really useful at this stage.

6   If you get the green light from the Head, then get together with any friends who are ready to help and any teachers who have offered support, to discuss what should happen at your first meeting. This is really, really massively important, because if you get off to a disorganised start then you'll find it hard to recover. The SchoolsLive website resources should be especially helpful at this stage (point 1 above).

7   Having organised it, you need to publicise it. Perhaps write personal invitations to all the Christians that you know in the school. (If you can provide free biscuits or food at the first meeting it may encourage a few more to come!)

8 When you've organised and publicised, all you can do is wait and pray! When the first meeting happens, someone needs to explain to the people there (and don't be discouraged if there are fewer than you'd hoped for) what the Christian group is all about and why it's important to have a group in school. The two main reasons are:

TO ENCOURAGE THE CHRISTIANS
and to
INTRODUCE ANY NON-CHRISTIANS TO JESUS.

9 Try to be as enthusiastic as possible (enthusiasm is catching!), take the names of everyone who came, and ask them if they know of any other Christians to invite to the next meeting.

10 Soon after the first meeting, get together with your planning group again and talk about what should happen next. (Again, the SchoolsLive resources will be very useful.)

Think about it

1 If Jesus came to your school:
(a) who would he feel pity for?
(b) who would he spend time with?
(c) who or what would upset him?
(d) who or what would please him?
(e) what would he say to your friends?

2 How like Jesus are YOU in school?

Outro

(Where do we go from here?)

Here are ten assorted uses for this book:

1 Rip it into tiny pieces and throw it at the bride and groom at the next wedding you see.
2 Put it in a food processor, add water and make Chocolate Teapot soup.
3 Sit on it all night.
4 Put it in your trainers and run round the garden.
5 Tie it to a stick and play badminton with it.
6 Take it back to the shop you bought it from and ask for your money back.
7 Put it in a DVD player and watch it.
8 Give it to someone you don't like very much.
9 Plant it in a Gro-bag and water it every day.
10 Introduce it to your pet gerbil.

Or you could read it and spend some time thinking about it! If you've read the book, go back and have a quick look at 'The really important bit' and the 'Think about it' section in each chapter. You'll probably find that there are some bits that you've almost forgotten already, but other bits are still quite fresh in your mind. In case you're wondering why that is, here's the reason!

When you read a book like this, God wants to speak to you through what it says. Don't forget that

God knows you inside out, so he knows what you need. As you've been reading this book, God has been telling the Holy Spirit to make the bits that are especially important for you to stick in your mind. So the parts you can remember are possibly the parts that God really wants you to hear AND DO SOMETHING ABOUT!

The real value of this book to you is if it helps you live more confidently as a Christian in school. God wants to help you do that, but you'll have to play your part. This book has given you quite a bit of practical advice – things to actually DO, but you can't do everything all at once. So start with just one thing – maybe your attitude to teachers, or your willingness to speak up for Jesus, whatever is a problem for you at the moment – and get stuck into sorting that one thing out. After a period of time you'll feel that things have improved a bit in that area (we hope!). Then flick through the book again and start trying to work at another area.

If you're normal, you won't have enjoyed this book much! But, apart from that, you'll also continue to get things wrong occasionally. Don't give up at the first mistake. Ask God to forgive you and help you start all over again. Don't be a chocolate teapot, melting away when the heat's turned up at school. Stand up for God and know that he loves you enough to help you through each day, however hot it gets.